Alfred Rimmer

Rambles Round Rugby

Alfred Rimmer

Rambles Round Rugby

ISBN/EAN: 9783337187293

Printed in Europe, USA, Canada, Australia, Japan

Cover: Foto ©ninafisch / pixelio.de

More available books at **www.hansebooks.com**

RAMBLES ROUND
RUGBY

BY ALFRED RIMMER

WITH AN INTRODUCTORY CHAPTER BY

THE REV. W. H. PAYNE SMITH, M.A.
ASSISTANT MASTER AT RUGBY SCHOOL

Old Quadrangle Rugby

WITH SEVENTY-THREE ILLUSTRATIONS BY THE AUTHOR

London
PERCIVAL & CO.
1892

PREFACE

IT is not proposed in this work to give an exhaustive account of any particular places or scenes, but rather to intimate and point out the interesting parts which may be most easily reached. The country round Rugby is rich in historical associations which have greatly influenced English history, for within reach the first and the last of Cromwell's battles were fought. The Wars of the Roses were ended here, and, so far as we know, this was one of the most important Roman centres of England.

But these are matters, perhaps, that ramblers in country lanes would not care so much to attend to when there are other things of more present interest, such wild-flowers and bushes and reeds.

As spring advances towards April the well-known Wake Robin, or Lords and Ladies (*Arum maculatum*), is common in the hedges, and its straight stems, with the single leaf at the top, are very graceful. It grows from a sort of cup under the ground that contains a quantity of starch. The 'self-heal,' which is said to be a very excellent cure for quinsy and cuts, the thyme-leaved veronica, and many others, now appear. The red and white campions send out a pleasant scent, and the foxglove, that has a pleasing record with boys, and countless others, bloom. The 'blue-bell of Scotland,' as it is called,—doubtless from the colour of the Stuart's ribbon,—is often in such immense quantities that a considerable patch of ground is quite coloured by it. But a very few weeks will commence a liking for botany, and when a little knowledge is accumulated, it soon becomes permanent and increases.

There are those who would feel more interest in insects and butterflies than plants, and for such the country round Rugby is a happy hunting-ground, and collections may be easily made. A microscope is a useful accompaniment, and shows us the wonders of these creatures. The eggs of butterflies are very singular; they differ as much, and even more than the creatures themselves, and that is saying a great deal. Then the stages of caterpillar, chrysalis, and imago are wonderful. The miniature organs of the wings may be traced in the caterpillar when only a few days old, and in the antennae are organs of sense of which we are entirely ignorant. If, for example, a virgin butterfly,—and this applies to many species,—is enclosed in a perforated box and placed where it can be seen, it draws admirers from great distances; but the strangest thing is, that when a companion is chosen the others retire, and if exposed again not a single one appears. This points to some sense of which we are quite ignorant, and with which none of our own correspond. The more we look into animated nature the more we shall see how little we know of any but a limited number of the senses on earth.

A collection of moths and butterflies may easily be made with a gauze net, and a small drop of ether secures the prize. The commonest of all butterflies is the 'white cabbage butterfly,' which does great havoc among green plants. It is, perhaps, the most difficult and wary of all to catch, yet in summer we hardly can travel many yards without its flitting across us. This species has very migratory habits, and will sometimes muster in large flocks and cross the sea. We find, also, in the lanes round Rugby, the 'blues' and the 'copper' and the 'brimstone' butterflies. We may also see in May the tortoise-shell butterflies, which fly in pairs, and are charming objects.

The 'Camberwell beauty' has once been found in the neighbourhood of Rugby; it selects the white willow to lay its eggs in. But those splendid butterflies, the 'red admiral' and the 'peacock,' are quite common. The latter may often be noticed resting with its wings open, and Taylor, in his *World of Mind*, suggests that this is done on purpose, that its beautiful adornments in which it delights may be in sight. Unlike other butterflies, the 'peacock' hybernates during the winter, and I have seen them in all their splendid plumage in early spring. The 'orange tip' and 'meadow brown' follow later, and are abundant in June and July.

There is what is sometimes called a nocturnal representative of the butterfly also in the same district, and some of the moths are nearly as beautiful as our butterflies. The Meadow Tiger, for example (*Chelonia caja*), has rich velvety fore wings, and the markings are cream coloured, the hind wings being beautifully red with fine black spots. Then we have the Hawk-moths with their long-sustained flights and mischievous lives. If, on a hot summer's day, you see a hedge stripped of its leaves for a considerable distance, and in it a sort of structure of cobweb appearance, the probability is that this contains the caterpillars of the small Eggar moth (*Eriogaster lanestris*). These caterpillars are black, unsightly things, and very much larger than the moth itself. Push the structure with your stick, and scores of similar caterpillars will come out and join their relatives who are engaged in desolating the hedge. Their way of life is rather amusing: they issue forth in single file at great length, and literally devour every green thing that comes in their way, and, singularly enough, they leave off feeding suddenly and return to their quarters. Still more mischievous is the Goat moth (*Cossus ligniperda*), the larva of which is a terrible destroyer of trees, boring holes in them, and making promenades that do not at all times show from the outside. I have seen a log of foreign timber sold that had no appearance externally of demolition, but, when it came under the sawyer's hands, it was found to be a perfect wreck. The larvae of the Goat moth are very large, and Pliny mentions them as a much-prized dish among the affluent Romans. It was looked upon as a great delicacy from its high flavour, and it was fattened on flour for some time before cooking. It would be impossible to give even a partial list of the many moths of the Rugby lanes. The butterflies, it may be said, rest with their wings closed and the moths with theirs open, though, of course, the 'peacock' and 'red admiral' will open and show their superb colours. The beetles are also full of interest, and the stag-beetle is not uncommon.

But the most charming of all live creatures in our rambles are the migratory and non-migratory birds. There are two kinds of migratory birds,—those which come in spring and stay until the end of summer, and those which leave their northern abodes and stay with us over the winter. To the former belong the well-known martin and swift, and all the swallow kind, which are looked forward to with great interest and welcome; and the cuckoo, which is more heard than seen, and tells us that spring has set in. Whether the nightingale reaches the neighbourhood I was never able to ascertain personally, but they say it does. Its habits are most unintelligible, and nothing we know of can account for them. The eggs have been frequently taken away from some place and put in another bird's nest in some district which they do not frequent. The food they are partial to has been sown, and, under skilled gardeners' hands, carefully brought to perfection; but instead of the young ones that had grown and prospered returning to the same district, they go to the place where their eggs were laid on their return to England the following year. Why should Devonshire, of all counties, be without nightingales? It is not generally known, but it is said, on the highest authority, that the blackbirds which abound in the lanes in winter are not English birds but foreign, from Denmark, Norway, and Sweden, and our own emigrate to milder lands in the South. The birds that spend their winter with us from other countries principally belong to the duck tribe. The absence of marsh lands round Rugby does not attract them, still they are met with on the Avon, and in the winter I have seen flights at some height up, and in considerable numbers, going probably to distant marsh lands.

The English wild duck is the most timid of all our birds, and the most difficult to approach; but I could mention a very singular circumstance I saw on the road on a spring day when going from Liverpool to Rugby. There is a duck decoy at a place called Hale, near Liverpool, that stands away from the road at the junction of two very large marshy fields. The Warrington railway runs very near it, and within two miles is the noisy Runcorn viaduct across the Mersey. The decoy pond covers five acres, and is surrounded with a high wooden boarding and trees; and outside the boarding is a wide, deep moat, which is crossed by a single locked drawbridge. In looking through a small nick in the boarding I saw some six hundred wild ducks, all at their ease. The keepers at Hale Hall say that the fields are quiet, and the loud railway whistles give no alarm at all; they are accustomed to them in the same way as we may see from an express train water-hens on a pool that take no notice of the furious passer-by.

But the summer birds of the green lanes and fields are the most interesting. The song of the lark, when the bird is invisible up in the air, is very delightful, and in early summer the lanes ring all over with the melodies of thrushes and blackbirds. The titmice are numerous in the lanes round Rugby, and I could count five different species; the bearded tit, the crested tit, the long-tailed tit, the great and the blue tits. Warblers and fly-catchers also abound in these lanes, and so do yellow-hammers and goldfinches, though these are less common everywhere than formerly, owing not to their being destroyed, but to the doing away with hedges where they got their food, and the substitution of wooden fences.

The green plover or lapwing forms a very amusing companion at laying-time, when it comes in front of any one that is near its nest, and with screams of distress allures the intruders away from its eggs. The lark, which also lays on the ground, has a very different way of dealing with them. Its back claw is especially long, and it can clip its eggs when in danger and fly away with them. This has often been seen. But the most beautiful of all English birds is not uncommon on the Avon, though very rare in some parts of England. The kingfishers, in their brilliant plumage, are little inferior to any foreign bird. They have a wide distribution over the earth, and this indicates a high geological antiquity. Those on the American rivers are considerably larger than ours, and not nearly so brilliant in colour. Kingfishers build their nests in holes on the bank of the river, and commonly choose the hole of the water-rat. They widen in, and build their nests of fish-bones some distance from the surface of the bank. Kites and hawks of various kinds are not so common as they were, owing to the deadly enmity of the keepers. But the little that has been said is enough to point out what objects of interest present themselves to the rambler.

Lastly, let me refer to the architectural beauties of the parish churches. These abound in Northampton, which, if we except Lincoln, has no rival in any English county. The dates of the windows may easily be learned, and the interest aroused is so great that the student soon begins to notice the various styles of mouldings, and the characteristics of styles. These never err or vary ; a single moulding will tell the date of the structure. Bloxam is one of our great authorities on architecture, and was a constant resident in Rugby during his long life.

ALFRED RIMMER.

January 1892.

CONTENTS

RUGBY.

PAGE

The Town of Rugby—The Church—The Old Church Tower—Lawrence Sheriff—Rugby School—Dr. Arnold—Archbishop Tait—Dean Goulburn—Bishop Temple—Dr. Hayman—Dr. Jex Blake—The School Chapel, ... 1-37

ASHBY ST. LEGERS: GUNPOWDER PLOT.

Approaches to Ashby St. Legers—Church at Ashby and preservation by the Lord of the Manor—Catesbys, Ratcliffes, and Lovells—Thomas Cromwell and his treatment of sequestered Abbots—Lady Catesby and her Son—Percy, his Co-conspirator—John Wright, his Ally, and the others—Tresham, and his Letter to Monteagle—James I. and his pretended connection with the Discovery of Guy Fawkes, ... 38-52

ASHBY ST. LEGERS AND SENHOUSE FAMILY.

Gathering Arms at Ashby—Princess Elizabeth to be placed on the Throne—Flight of Conspirators—Dunchurch—Arrival of Conspirators at Ashby—Holbeach, the Seat of Stephen Littleton, besieged—Execution of Conspirators—Ashby St. Legers Hall—Tulip Tree—Irving Family, and Pocklington Senhouse and Family—Sir Everard Digby, ... 53-60

CRICK CHURCH AND NEIGHBOURHOOD.

Crick Church—Watford Court—Lord Northington—Battle of Bosworth—Extinction of the House of Plantagenet, . . . 61-71

EDGEHILL AND NASEBY.

Battle of Edgehill—Charles at Nottingham—Prince Rupert—Lord Brooke—Shuckburgh—Kineton—Radway—Lord Lindsay—Green's History of the Battle—Lord Fairfax—Issues between the King and the People—Destruction of Antiquities through Charles—Naseby—King Charles's Tower, Chester—Uxbridge Council—Montrose—Naseby Battlefield—Marston Trussel Church—Old Account of Battle, ... 72-88

COVENTRY.

Ryton-on-Dunsmore — Coventry Spires—Coventry— Damage by Charles II. after Restoration, and Destruction of Walls—Gosford Green, and the Scene of Meeting for Combat between Bolingbroke and Norfolk—River Avon—Baginton—Continuation of Meeting between Bolingbroke and Norfolk—Coventry Cross, and English Crosses—St. Mary's Hall—St. Michael's Church—Holy Trinity Church—Greyfriars' Hospital—Coventry Parliaments, ... 89-105

WARWICK.

Remarks on English Architecture—Italian Substitution—Chester Walls—Leicester's Hospital—Nilometer—St. Mary's Church and Beauchamp Chapel—Leicester and Amy Robsart—Cumnor Hall—Inquest—Anthony Foster—Stoneleigh Abbey—Leigh Family — Lord Ellesmere — Cistercian Monks — Radmore — Guy's Cliff—Guy, Earl of Warwick—Guy's Cliff Mill, . . 106-122

STONELEIGH ABBEY.

Stoneleigh Abbey—Abbots—Fire at Abbey—English Architecture—Churches round Rugby and Northampton—Greek Architecture—Theory of painted Temples—Valuation of Abbey Revenues at Dissolution—Royal Commission on Dissolution—The 'Black Book'—Ashow—Baginton—Whitley Abbey—Stivichall—Road from Rugby to Coombe—Murder of Sir Theodosius Boughton—Newbold-on-Avon—Church Lawford (King's Newnham)—Dr. Buckland and Remains of extinct Animals—Binley—Brinklow—Oxford Canal—Roman Fosse—Coombe Abbey—Abbey Lands and Lake—Deer Park—Elizabeth, Queen of Bohemia—Dissolution of Abbey—Alms and Hospitality—Road to Market Harboro'—Rutland County—Leicestershire roads—Watling Street—Leicester part of see of Lincoln, and afterwards Peterboro'—Leicester cattle and Stilton cheese—Stanford—Stanford Church—The Cave Family—Baron Braye—Stanford Hall—Cave killed by Biron—River Avon—South Kilworth—North Kilworth—Husbands Bosworth—Turville family—Sir Wm. Turville, an Ecclesiastical Commissioner—Theddingworth—Lubbenham—Holdenby—Welford—East Haddon—Removal of Charles from Holdenby—Sale of Holdenby House—John of Padua—Theobalds, ... 123-173

MARKET HARBORO'.

Market Harboro'—Little Bowden—Great Bowden—Sutton Bassett—Weston by Welland—Ashley—Leicester Archæological Society—Roman Remains—Market Harboro' Church—Rockingham—Pipewell Abbey—Rockingham Castle—Caldicott approach to district from Uppingham—Great Easton—Bradley Priory—Rockingham Hostel—Lyddington—Lyddington Church and Palace—Cardinal Wolsey—Grossteste and the Pope—Snelston—Lord Burleigh—Palace converted to a Hospital for the Aged—Wing—Manton—Thorney Abbey—Oakham—Thomas Cromwell—Baron of Oakham—Ferrars Family—Poll Tax and Ormskirk—Flore's House—Reversions of Oakham—Piers Gaveston—Hudson the Dwarf—Burleigh Hall—Stamford and its Architecture—Edmund Ironside—Bridge over Welland—Dickens on Stamford—Eleanor Cross—Henry Cecil, Earl of Exeter, divorced and married Miss Hoggins—Beautiful Ballad by Tennyson—Burleigh House and Pictures—Verrio and Lagerre—Paintings at Burleigh—Thackeray on great mansions—Lake—Attacks on Burleigh House in Civil War—William Cecil—Queen Elizabeth's Ely letter—John Thorpe, Elizabethan Architect—Dr. Stukeley, Vicar of All Saints, ... 174-220

BILTON.

Bilton—Bilton Hall—Dutch Gardens—Addison, his early life and career—Addison's father—Amesbury and Salisbury Plain—Bustards—Addison's father, Dean of Lichfield—Addison's knowledge of Latin—Fellow of Magdalen—His upward career

	PAGE
— His Poem on Marlboro' Gale of 1703—Purchased Bilton Hall —Sir Roger de Coverley—Ayston Church—Preston Church— Bilton Church—Bilton Grange—Dunchurch—Pipewell Abbey —Dunchurch Stocks—Chancellor Eldon and the Stocks,	221-239

KENILWORTH.

From Stoneleigh to Kenilworth—English Castles—Leamington— Amy Robsart—Earl of Leicester—Early Architecture of Kenilworth—Kenilworth Lake—Gatehouse—Havoc by Parliamentarians—Geoffrey de Clinton—Pope Innocent—Simon de Montfort—Occupation of Kenilworth by John of Gaunt—General Destruction of Building—Lutterworth—Wycliffe—Papacy at Avignon—Lollards—Denial of Transubstantiation—Persecution of Wycliffe, and the unearthing of his remains to cast in the river Swift—Roman remains in England—Villas and roads, 240-265

LIST OF ILLUSTRATIONS

		PAGE
Rugby School,	Frontispiece.	
Old Quadrangle, Rugby,	Vignette on Title.	
River Avon, Rugby,		2
Rugby Mill,		3
Mill at Rugby,		12
Brownsover Cottage,		13
Old Quadrangle, Rugby,		28
Rugby School Chapel,		36
Ashby St. Legers Church, from the Park,		39
Ashby St. Legers (Church Windows),		41
Gunpowder Plot House,		43
Digby Monument, Stoke Dry,		48
Ashby St. Legers (Residence),		56
The Tulip Tree,		57
Crick Church (South-East),		61
Crick Church (Spire, etc.),		62
Blue Boar Tavern,		66
Edge Hill,		72
Warwick Castle,		78
Market Harboro', from Brewery Fields,		84
Naseby Church,		86
Coventry, Entrance Gate,		91

List of Illustrations.

	PAGE
CHURCH, ETC., AT COVENTRY,	93
HOLY TRINITY SPIRE, COVENTRY, .	101
GREY FRIARS' HOSPITAL, COVENTRY,	103
LEICESTER'S HOSPITAL, WARWICK, .	108
LEICESTER'S HOSPITAL (ANOTHER VIEW),	110
GUY'S CLIFF MILL, .	121
STONELEIGH ABBEY,	125
NEWNHAM REGIS, .	139
BRINKLOW TOWER, .	141
BRINKLOW TO RUGBY, .	142
IN COOMBE ABBEY PARK,	143
COOMBE ABBEY, WARWICK,	144
IN COOMBE ABBEY PARK, .	146
LEICESTER—ST. MARY'S CHURCH, .	149
LEICESTER—ST. MARGARET'S, .	151
LEICESTER—HOLY TRINITY HOSPITAL, .	151
WATLING STREET, .	152
STANFORD CHURCH,	155
STANFORD HALL, . .	158
SOUTH KILWORTH CHURCH, .	159
SOUTH KILWORTH, . . .	160
ON ROAD TO SOUTH KILWORTH, .	160
NORTH KILWORTH CHURCH, .	161
THEDDINGWORTH CHURCH, .	163
REMAINS OF HOLMBY HOUSE,	168
HOLMBY, ...	170
ENTERING MARKET HARBORO' FROM LEICESTER ROAD,	174
IN MARKET HARBORO', . .	177

List of Illustrations. xxiii

	PAGE
ROCKINGHAM,	183
ROCKINGHAM CHURCH,	187
MANTON,	196
WING MILL, RUTLAND,	198
OAKHAM, RUTLAND,	199
ALL SAINTS, STAMFORD,	208
BILTON HALL, RUGBY,	222
PRESTON CHURCH CHANCEL,	230
BILTON CHURCH, RUGBY,	231
ENTERING DUNCHURCH,	233
DUNCHURCH PARISH CHURCH,	235
THE STOCKS, DUNCHURCH,	236
IN DUNCHURCH,	238
KENILWORTH CASTLE, PORTER'S LODGE,	242
KENILWORTH CASTLE,	243
LUTTERWORTH CHURCH,	253
BRANDON,	258
WOLSTON,	259
WOLSTON CHURCH, RUGBY,	260
CLAYBROOKE CHURCH,	261
AT ULLESTHORPE,	262
AT ULLESTHORPE (ANOTHER VIEW),	263

RAMBLES ROUND RUGBY

RUGBY

HE who casts his eye on a map of Britain in the olden days, when it was a portion of the Roman Empire, will readily note the lines of the two chief Roman roads and the point, almost in the centre of the island, where they cross one another. The Stratum, or Watling Street, ran from London through the Midlands to Uriconium or Wroxeter; the Fossa, or Fosse Way, took its undeviating course from Aquae Solis, or Bath, to Lincoln. The ancient Roman station at the point of intersection now goes by the name of High Cross, and is marked by a pillar erected in the reign of Queen Anne, with an inscription denoting the historical interest of the position and also the restoration of peace to the kingdom. Some eight or ten miles south of this point, the Warwickshire Avon, flowing in this part of its course almost due west, cuts across both roads, and forms the base of a triangle having the two roads as its sides and High Cross at its apex. On the Avon, about mid-way between the two roads, lies the town of Rugby, in the midst of pleasant, gentle, meadow scenery, with splendid trees scattered plentifully on all sides in field and hedge-row.

Amidst minor effects which Arnold's influence at Rugby, or that of Stanley's famous biography of him, produced, there may be counted a depreciation of

Warwickshire scenery. The passage is well known, in which his feelings are described: (*Life of Arnold*, i. p. 210): 'The monotonous character of the midland scenery of Warwickshire was to him, with his strong love of natural beauty and variety, absolutely repulsive; there was something almost touching in the eagerness with which, amidst that "endless succession of fields and hedge-rows," he would make the most of any features of a higher order; in the pleasure with which he would cherish the few places where the current of the Avon was perceptible, or where a glimpse of the horizon could be discerned; in the humorous despair with which he would gaze on the dull expanse of fields eastward from Rugby. It is no wonder that we do not like looking that way, when one considers that there is nothing fine between us and the Ural Mountains. Conceive what you look over, for you must miss Sweden, and look over Holland, the north of Germany, and the centre of Russia."' To persons who can see beauties in scenery, even if it possesses no mountains, or who have not such a vivid imagination as to grieve because an eastward gaze, if it could see far enough, would miss the Valdai

Hills and descry only the flatter centre of Russia, such lamentations seem exaggerated. Warwickshire has its own beauty, and a very peaceful and restful, if not exciting, kind of beauty it is; it is found in the bright greenness of meadows, the graceful masses of foliage of

the splendid timber, the glimpses of the sluggish Avon among the trees, and the succession of many a rounded knoll crowned with grand elms and beeches, with the old-world cottage roofs nestling along the sloping road, and the tower or spire of the village church peeping out among the trees. The traveller need not go far from Rugby to find many a spot on which the eye lingers with delight; the woods of Coombe, the meanderings of the Avon in the deep meadows near Bretford and Wolston, the stately beeches at Stanford, or the grand avenue, some three miles of Scotch firs and three more of elms, along the road across Dunsmore Heath. But there are many signs that the midland scenery of England is beginning to be more rightly appreciated in the present day; we can turn back to Rugby without further defence of it.

Situated as it is so close to the two great roads, within easy reach of many an old British or Roman station or earthwork, Rugby itself retains scarcely any link with the distant past. A few pieces of Roman and Saxon pottery, an old dagger or two, and one or two other relics, are all that the past has given up.[1] But there are also visible two old tumuli, one in the School Close (the well-known 'Island' famous in the story of *Tom Brown*, of which more anon), the other in a field on the western side of Rugby, adjoining the Lawford Road. These two mounds take us back to times anterior to the Roman conquest of Britain; they mark the time when the Avon was the boundary line

---

[1] The articles referred to came for the most part into the possession of the great Rugby antiquary, the late M. H. Bloxam, Esq., F.S.A., etc., and were left by him to the Rugby School Art Museum, where they may now be seen.

between the British tribes of the Dobuni and Coritani (or Coritavi), and might enable a vivid imagination to picture somewhat of the doings of these shadowy folk. Here, in the Island, combining it may be sentiment with practical use, the Dobuni raised a tumulus over the bones of some old warrior, and raised it in such a spot as to form one of the links in the chain of posts which acted as a defence for their northern frontier, and as signal stations along which the news might speed of any hostile movements on the part of their foes.

A long step must next be taken. Domesday Book, of course, records what Rugby was at the time of the Norman Conquest. *Rocheberie* (so was the name then spelt, which, after passing through the forms of Rochebe and Rokeby, appears at last in Leland's writings as Rugby) was then a manor or demesne of little importance, the superior lord of which was Turchel de Warwick, and which was held under him by a family who took from the place the name of De Rokeby. It possessed no church of its own, being, in fact, a 'member' of the neighbouring parish of Clifton, which it afterwards outstripped in growth and progress. It is not till some fifty years later than Domesday Book that we have definite record of the existence of a chapel at Rugby. Early in the thirteenth century, through the exertions of Henry de Rokeby, Rugby was separated from Clifton, and the chapel was converted into a parish church. Those who are curious in such matters can see an elaborate account of the matter in the late Mr. M. H. Bloxam's *Rugby*, pp. 119 to 138. With his usual painstaking accuracy, he collected every notice in existence of the history of the church and parish of Rugby; his writings, indeed, form the quarry from which every subsequent writer on Rugby must hew such material as he wants. The matter is too elaborate and technical for our present purpose: it must suffice to say that no part exists in the present church which takes us back to these early dates. The earliest existing building in Rugby is the old church-tower, which, together with four arches inside the church, is all that remains of work erected prior to the Reformation. This old tower stands at the western end of the church, and is remarkable for more than one reason. It is remarkable, first, for the difficulty which has been experienced in dating it. An observer so competent as Mr. Bloxam,—than whom no one ever possessed wider knowledge and experience of the characteristics of mediæval buildings,—was puzzled by it. It is known that the second Henry de Rokeby, son of the one alluded to above, and inheritor of his frequent disputes with the Abbey of Leicester as to rights over the church and living of Rugby, built a chancel in the Early English style (he lived in the reign of Henry III.), which existed till the year 1814. The nave and aisles were erected later, probably by Ralph, Lord Stafford, about A.D. 1350. To which of these periods did the tower belong? Mr. Bloxam appears at first to have thought that it belonged to the earlier time, but in later writings ascribed it more confidently to the later, *i.e.* to the middle of the fourteenth century. Others, with more dogmatism than discretion, have made up a theory that this tower was erected a hundred years or so earlier, and was intended by the Rokeby family to take the place of the castle, which had been originally erected in the troublous days of Stephen, and subsequently with many others dismantled by order of Henry II. This brings us to the second noteworthy point about the tower. It has not the aspect of an ecclesiastical edifice, so much as of one intended for a warlike stronghold: it is very solid, nearly square, possessing originally no entrance except on the inside from the church, and in the lower portions it has no windows, but only sundry very narrow slits, like the loopholes of a castle, at a considerable distance from the ground.

In recent years the church has been rebuilt on a much larger scale, and this tower at the present day has a somewhat forlorn and depressed look, dwarfed as it is by the height and magnitude of the present edifice. But the town has grown so rapidly in the present century that even this enlarged church would have been wholly insufficient for the needs of the place. A second church, that of the Holy Trinity, has been erected as belonging to the mother-parish, while two separate districts, those of St. Matthew, Rugby, and New Bilton, each with its own church, have been formed on the west and south sides of the town.

The following particulars, gathered from Nicolas' *History of Rugby*, pp. 75, fol., possess some interest. About A.D. 1562, 'the housholde' of Rugby amounted to sixty-nine. One hundred years later there were 160 houses in the parish. At the census of 1801 there were 1487 inhabitants; twenty years later the number was 2300; at the present time there are between eleven and twelve thousand. There still live persons who can remember the time when Rugby was but a little village, with the postmark of 'Rugby, near Dunchurch,' when the present Schoolhouse and Old Big School were just completed, and when along the unlighted and unpaved streets there were scarcely twenty houses in existence of those which compose the present town. Various causes have contributed to the change. In early times Rugby owed what little business and trade it had to its various fairs, for the sale of cattle and other purposes. These still flourish, but the growth of the place has been due to two causes, one, the great development of the school at the end of the last century, and in the first half of the present one; the other, the advent in 1838 of the L. and N.-W. Railway, which has made the despised 'Mugby Junction' portrayed by Dickens into one of the busiest spots in England, with a splendid island-platform a quarter of a mile long, an unceasing rush and roar of mighty trains, and a host of railwaymen who dwell in the neat streets which have sprung up in the vicinity of the railway. In fact, it might be said with rough accuracy that Rugby now consists of three zones; first, on the slope of ground towards the Avon and the railway come the employés of the line, in the middle a district of business-men and auctioneers, and them that have to do with horses—for Rugby is a great hunting centre, and the branch establishment of the great Tattersall firm finds here its home; thirdly, at the upper end of the town, toward the open country, comes the school, with its boarding-houses and tradesmen, and various dependants.

Not to the Rugbeian alone is the name of Rugby

dear for the sake of the school. Rugby School occupies in some respects a position of its own amongst the great schools of England. After some 200 years of comparative insignificance, various causes contributed to foster its growth. When it had grown to fair stature, the man came to it whose work, and fame, and influence were, and are unrivalled. The names of Rugby and of Arnold are inseparable. Through him a new spirit was breathed into English public schools; the impress of his character was such that pupils and colleagues were proud to cherish it as their best possession; through many of them Rugby became the mother of many of the noble schools which have sprung up in the last fifty years to a vigour and success which equals her own. Cotton and Bradley at Marlborough, Benson at Wellington, Butler at Haileybury, Percival at Clifton; these all, besides other less notable examples, served their apprenticeship at, and drew their inspiration from, the Rugby of Arnold and his successors. It may be interesting to trace some of the steps by which the originally modest foundation of Lawrence Sheriff grew great.

We must turn our thoughts back to the days when Rugby was a tiny village, far from the bustle of the world, with its scattered wooden houses frequently subject to grievous fires, and its stocks and pillory and ducking-stool, for the discouragement of the evil-minded or scolding-tongued, and for the preservation of order and morals within its borders. Here, at some unknown date in the earlier years of the Tudors, Lawrence Sheriff saw the light, in a house opposite to the parish church, and with windows looking out towards the tower which has been described above. Of his early life little enough is known. How, or why, or when he settled in London we do not know, but there we find him, in the reign of Edward VI., a prosperous grocer in Newgate Street, a royal tradesman, and devoted to the Princess (afterwards Queen) Elizabeth. The household accounts of the princess in the years 1551-52 are extant, and under the head of 'The Spicerie and Chaundrye' occur constant entries of sums paid to Lawrence Shreffe, Sherif, Shrefe, and so on (it would be difficult to devise a way of spelling his name which does not there occur), for spices and necessaries. A little later there is a grant of a coat of arms, a record of the interchange of new year's gifts between him and the queen, election to the Vice-Wardenship of the Grocer's Company, and the facts of his life are almost at an end without anything which shows us what manner of man Lawrence was. Besides his will, however, there remains one incident recorded in Foxe's *Book of Martyrs*, which throws a bright light on the fearless loyalty and courage of the man. It was in the reign of Queen Mary, soon after 'the stir of Wiat,' that Lawrence went one morning into the Rose Tavern for a drink and a gossip. It fortuned that at that moment one Robert Farrer was in the tavern with three companions. The account speaks in no kindly terms of this man; it avers that 'he was seldom absent from this tavern,' and plainly hints that on this morning he had taken too 'full cups.' So it came to pass that he had not consideration who were present, and spoke roughly of the Princess Elizabeth, among other courtesies calling her a Jill, and expressing a hope that she and her adherents should 'hop headless, or be fried with faggots,' before she should come to the crown. This was more than Sheriff could stand; he maintained the princess' cause boldly, called his whilom friend a knave, and declared that he would complain of him to the commission, then sitting at Bishop Bonner's house beside St. Paul's. 'Do thy worst,' said Farrer, 'for that I said, I will say again.' He had a truer appreciation of the likelihood of the commission upholding the cause of the Princess Elizabeth than his adversary. When Sheriff came before them, the commissioners made excuses for Farrer, and when the accuser was importunate, sent him away with a vague promise that they would rebuke the ribald frequenter of the Rose.

There were easier and less anxious times for Sheriff when his royal mistress came to the throne, but he only lived to see the first nine or ten years of her reign. In the year 1567 sickness came upon him, and on July 22 he made his will, being then, as he describes himself, 'sick of body, but of good and perfect remembrance, for which thanked be God.' In it he provided for his burial in the parish church of St. Andrew, in Rugby, and then proceeded to specify various charitable and kindly bequests to the parish and town, to his relations, and to sundry maids, apprentices, and friends. His wish, however, as regards his burial was not carried out; his body was interred in Christ Church, Newgate Street, which church perished in the great fire of London, A.D. 1666. Now comes the portion of the will in which he provided for the foundation of a school in his native village. For that purpose, with which he combined the endowment of some alms-houses, he left to certain trustees his land, tenements, etc., in the county of Warwick, together with the sum of £100 for the purchase of more land. These lands consisted of two parts: first, the rectory of Brownsover; secondly, the house in Rugby in which the founder was born, and which he inherited from his father. This was an old timber building, and stood on the site of the eastern-

most alms-houses; the site and premises were small, comprising less than half an acre in all. Here the school was carried on for nearly two centuries, until the time of the move to its present site in 1750.

Attached to the will was a document entitled 'the Intent of Lawrence Sheriff,' which approaches more nearly than anything else to the character of original statutes for the school. In it the founder states his wishes with regard to the school; 'a fayre and convenyent schoole howse' is to be built on to the dwelling-house, and four alms-houses to be erected near it; the trustees are to 'cause an honest, discreete, and learned man, being a Master of Arts, to be reteyned to teach a Free Grammar School in the said schoole house,' chiefly for the children of Rugby and Brownsover, but not to the exclusion of such as be of other places thereunto adjoining; the master is to have the dwelling-

Brownsover Cottage

house for his residence, and a salary of £12 a year. A few weeks later, and only a fortnight or so before his death, Sheriff journeyed to Rugby and there executed a codicil to his will, which was afterwards of the utmost importance to the school. Some years previously he had purchased for £320 twenty-four acres of land in the outskirts of London, in Lamb's Conduit Fields. Wherefore, or for what object he made the change is unknown, but he now revoked the legacy of £100 to be laid out in land, and substituted for it one third part of this property in Middlesex. We shall trace shortly the importance of this codicil.

It may seem at first sight scarcely worth while to enter into these details as to the foundation of the school. But the whole matter was one very characteristic of the times. England is dotted over with schools, many of which, in their early history, bear close resemblance to Rugby; some have grown to be great, others have remained—as for many generations it seemed likely that Rugby would—humble places dealing out a little learning to the few children of the village or town in which they stand. The time of the Tudors was an era of school-founding. Two causes led to this. One lay in the general influence of the renascence of learning; the treasures of Greek and Latin literature had been unearthed, the universities had once more become the homes of ardent scholars, whose own pursuit of, and delight in, learning filled them with a desire to promote the education of youth. Such was notably Dean Colet, who founded St. Paul's School in 1509, in the face of loud outcries from opponents who hated the reformed methods of education. Imitators followed in crowds. 'More grammar schools, it has been said, were founded in the latter years of Henry VIII. than in the three centuries before.' (Green's *History*, p. 305.) The second cause which contributed to this was the dissolution of the monasteries. Many of them had served as schools; their disappearance made a need for new ones, and their property provided means to meet the need. Edward VI. and Elizabeth followed in the same path, founding many more grammar schools. And in the reign of the latter private individuals took their part in the good work. Such were notably John Lyon, yeoman, the founder of Harrow, and Lawrence Sheriff, grocer, of Rugby.

Behold, then, the free school of the worthy grocer established in the founder's house. For several generations its history presents but little interest; it is a miserable record of quarrels about the property. Some of Sheriff's relatives, notably a nephew born some few years after the foundation, tried to appropriate the property of the school; litigation ensued, and it was not till just one hundred years after Sheriff's death that final judgment was given, securing its own to the school, and driving off the harpies. The names of one or two masters in this period are known, and little else; the position was not an enviable one, money was short, in one year only two shillings and sevenpence were forthcoming in lieu of the salary of £12.

The school might have continued for ever nothing more than a little local free school, but for one or two noteworthy incidents, which enlarged its fame and brought it into a condition fitted to profit by the enormous increase in the value of the London estates. There does not seem much connection between Rugby and the arbitrary attempt of King James II. to force Anthony Farmer as President on Magdalen College, Oxford. But there was at that time, among the chaplains of the college, one Henry Holyoak, a Warwickshire man by birth, and very likely a friend of one of the Demies, Richard Adams, who had been educated at Rugby School. In 1687 these two, along with President, Fellows, and other Demies and Chaplains, were ejected from the college, and their places were supplied by Roman Catholics according to the king's orders. The mastership of Rugby School was vacant at the time, and to it Henry Holyoak was elected, and though restored to his chaplaincy at Magdalen in the next year, 1688, he stuck to the school and remained headmaster till 1730, a period of nearly forty-four years.

The school must have been little more than a name or a shadow when he came to it. Robert Ashbridge, master twelve years before, had been a successful man, and had started the Rugby School Register; he had admitted as many as twenty-six boys in one year, and had attracted several pupils from a little distance. But his successor, Leonard Jeacock, was not a success; the register reveals the fact that he admitted only two boys in 1683, and in 1684 only one, while for 1685 there is no entry at all. However, with Holyoak came a change; he was an accomplished scholar, descended from a family of scholars—well known, no doubt, through the part he took in the famous affair of Magdalen College—a man of a genial and popular disposition, as is testified to by the fact that no less than three livings in the neighbourhood were presented to him while at Rugby. Boys soon began to come to the school. In his forty-three years there are no less than 630 entries, of whom 500 came from a distance and only 130 were foundationers. The school became popular with the clergy and gentry of its own and the neighbouring counties. The question could not but arise, Was the school to be continually confined to the narrow boundaries of the founder's house, or must something be done to enlarge its borders?

It is a matter for regret that no trace remains of the old mansion; it has long since fallen, and no picture or drawing of it remains. The only description of it, indeed—and that but a rough one—is contained in an often-quoted letter written in 1809 to the *Gentleman's Magazine* by one who had been taught in it sixty years before. 'The original school-room at Rugby (he says) in which I received the first part of my education under Dr. Knail, was a long, rather lofty room, built with timber, opposite the church. The house was very indifferent. I have said many a lesson in a small room into which the doctor occasionally called some boys, and in which he smoked many a pipe, the fragrance of which was abundantly retained in the blue cloth hangings with which it was fitted up. On the anniversary, which was in the summer, the school was strewed with rushes, the trustees attended, and speeches were made by several of the boys, some in Latin, some in English. . . . The general number of scholars was, in my time, I think, under seventy; but which number has since been very greatly increased. I do not recollect any playground belonging to the old school, but there was a piece of ground beyond the churchyard sometimes used by them. There were several almsmen who used to attend prayers in blue gowns.'

A few years after Holyoak's death Thomas Crossfield was elected to the mastership, being the thirteenth holder of that office whose name is recorded. He was a man of high reputation, as his epitaph in the parish church records, '*fama præeunte et commendante splendidæ dux coloniæ huc migravit.*' This 'splendid colony' consisted of the number—for that period very remarkable—of fifty boarders, whom he brought with him, and for whom accommodation had to be found in the town. The career so auspiciously begun was cut short by death only two years later, but the circumstances pressed on the question which was calling for solution, viz., how was the growing fame and magnitude of the school to be provided for in the narrow premises which had been its home since 1567.

The immense importance of the codicil to the founder's will now began to be apparent. What had been land of little value in the 'outskirts' of London, was now becoming, or had become, building-land of great and ever-growing value. It is true that in the Act of Parliament which was procured in 1748, it is stated that the annual income of the charity was at that date only £116 odd ; but it was a time of great expectations. The long leases on which the London property was let were not to fall in for another thirty years or so ; but it was quite safe to borrow. It may be observed in passing that when the leases did fall in, in 1777, a new Act of Parliament was passed regulating the disposal of the now much increased income, providing for the appointment of ushers, and among other points instituting for the first time exhibitions tenable for seven years. In later years the income of the charity increased still further, and rose at last to the value of some six or seven thousand a year. So great were the results of the mysterious codicil!

But to return to the Act of 1748. In it the school is stated to have been for many years past in great repute, but the buildings had got into so ruinous a condition as to be incapable of repair. Power was given to the trustees to purchase a 'large and convenient new-built house,' and a parcel of ground, contiguous to the school premises, or, failing this, to purchase some other ground in the vicinity, and to adapt it to the use of the school. It was a critical moment. For some unknown reason the purchase of the house referred to could not be completed. At the same moment there was fortunately in the market the so-called manor house on the south side of the town, with eight acres of land attached to it. A Mr. Wm. Hiorn, architect, of Warwick, was employed to survey and report on the manor house. His report was favourable, both as to the structure itself and as to the possibility of converting it into premises suitable for a school. 'I believe,' he added, 'a house equally good, large, and commodious cou'd not be newly erected under the sum of two thousand Pounds, wherefore, in my apprehension, it is very well worth the Sum of one thousand Pounds, the Price demanded.'

So the purchase was completed, a schoolroom was built, and the school migrated in 1750 to its present quarters. Its history was uneventful till, in 1778, an Etonian, Thomas James, D.D., was elected to the headmastership. The school increased by leaps and bounds. The number of scholars under him at one time is said to have been 240. Rugby definitely took its place among the great schools of England. In this regime a new schoolroom was built, and a line of barn-like buildings, stretching towards the Dunchurch Road, was fitted up for teaching purposes. A very curious and interesting print exists, the work of Mr. Edward Pretty, drawing-master to the school, in 1809, which gives a faithful picture of these buildings as they stood just previous to their complete demolition. On the right are seen the gables of the old manor house; adjoining it a stately schoolroom with a semi-circular end towards the close, and a turret with bell and clock at the other end, arising above 'a handsome porch according to the rules of the Doric order.' Then came other schoolrooms with dormitories above, followed by the long row of barn-like buildings already mentioned. One of these rooms, known as 'over school,' with a bedroom, entitled 'Paradise,' opening into it, was often the scene of plays acted by the boys. Here William Charles Macready seems to have made some of his earliest appearances as an actor. His powers were early noted. When only fifteen years old the celebrated tragedian performed the part of Hamlet in the 'Closet Scene' at the Rugby speeches. In fact, these buildings must have been better suited to a remarkable ceremony, which from time to time took place in them, than to teaching. Merit was rewarded by the boys in an original manner a hundred years ago. A boy promoted into a new form was honoured by his new mates with the process of being 'chaired,' not unaccompanied with pinches in the softer portions of his person: to another form entry entailed 'buffeting,' *i.e.* running the gauntlet. For promotion into the fifth form was reserved the reward which Mr. Bloxam thus describes: 'The patient had to undergo the operation of "clodding," as it was called. Clods of plastic soil were prepared by fags from the slimy banks of the square pool. These were kneaded into balls, and dried ready for action. The noviciates of the fifth form had then to run the gauntlet along the sheds, and were pelted at by their elders in the fifth form, according to custom.' One can sympathise with the relief with which the venerable antiquary remarked that he was old enough to remember, though not to have endured, these processes. In his time promotion entailed no worse result than that the happy boy should treat his friends in his own boarding-house to a 'spread.'

The eight acres of land purchased with the manor house—the northern portion of the present glorious close with its green turf and noble elms—were not without a past history and interest. At the time of the purchase they were cut up into different fields by hedges, the lines of which are for the most part marked by the elms still standing. Next to the school building came Garden Close and Barn Close, then Pond Close stretching right across from the Barby to the Dunchurch Road. In the middle of this latter close stood the Grange of the monks of Pipewell, an old house surrounded by a moat, belonging in pre-reformation times to the monks of the great Abbey of Pipewell in Northamptonshire, to whom Henry de Rokeby had made a grant of some land in Rugby. The last vestiges of this moat were not filled up till 1816. In the corner towards the Barby Road stood the island, then a genuine island, with a moat some twenty feet or more broad round it, which a wooden drawbridge with a spiked gate in the centre crossed. Many a strange scene has the old island beheld, since the Dobuni lit their beacon-fires on it two thousand years ago. The moat may have been dug round it to turn it into a place of refuge in the wild reign of Stephen. Then the more peaceful monks enlarged it as a stew for their fish. After a blank of 500 years in its history we find it the central point of the tragi-comedy of Rugby's great rebellion in the reign of Dr. Ingles, who succeeded to Dr. James. After a glorious bonfire of benches, desks, and books, the rebels found the opposing army approaching to the attack, in the shape of a body of dealers who happened to be attending the great November horse-fair, reinforced by a party of soldiers then recruiting in the town. The incident recalls to mind the graphic account which the father of history gives of the ending of the revolt of their slaves against the Scythians. 'What are we doing, Scythians?' said one of them; 'take my advice, lay spear and bow aside, and let each man fetch his horsewhip, and go boldly up to them:' and the slaves ran away. So the boys, though the headmaster had shut himself up in his study, when they saw Mr. William Butlin, banker, advancing at the head of his troop of horse-dealers, armed with their formidable whips, bethought them of their inevitable fate, retreated hastily to the island, and soon surrendered. The consequences naturally were such that many of the rebels afterwards felt it 'too sore and painful a subject ever to allude to it.'

'Island fagging!' The very sound of the words calls up to Rugbeian minds the thought of Tom Brown and Scud East racing across the close, of Bishop Cotton and Arthur lying on the sward and talking over Arnold's wise and patient rule, and the explanation of the half-decayed remnants of gymnastic poles which still survive among the trees. The honoured author of *Tom Brown* has recently written an account in a school magazine of the custom—and a marvellous institution it was. One scarcely wonders that the American boy, when he has read of the fagging of olden days, thanks Providence that the Declaration of Independence made fagging impossible in the schools of the great Republic. It appears that before boarding-houses were built along the Barby Road, many boys had gardens in that region, and it was one of the fashions on speech-day for the visitors to inspect these plots. This garden procession must be preserved, so the gardens were transferred to the uncongenial soil of the island. Behold, then, on some chill afternoon in March, the sixth, after calling over, proclaiming 'Island fagging.' The row of fags is drawn up under the elms at the other end of the close; the signal to start is given, and the first six to reach the moat are let off. Six more, the first who volunteer to jump across, or rather to jump into, the moat, are excused; the rest are set to work to scratch with knives or sticks or broken fives-bats the plots assigned to different members of the sixth. After a few afternoons of this 'digging,' comes scene 2. 'Turf-cart' comes into use; a number of fags are harnessed to the car, and roll it along to some spot where turf to lay down between the beds can be procured. Then comes the order to the fags to 'plant flowers.' It is worse than the fate of the Israelites and their brick-making. However, youthful consciences are not always scrupulous in such little matters. To grow flowers in the island would be an insane idea; the only plan is to appropriate them ready grown from somebody's garden, will he nill he, and stick them into their places so short a time before speech-day, that they have not time to wither. Then comes the great garden procession, and kindly visitors have to tell their little fibs, and to hide their smiles as they congratulate the lordly masters of the ragged turf and drooping primroses on their horticultural success.

The change of speech-day from Easter to the summer put an end to this comedy in 1835. It was not till after Arnold's time that the close grew to its present fair proportions. At the time of the purchase of the property the close was surrounded on three sides by common land, called Rugby Field. This was enclosed in 1774, and portions of it were allotted to those who had rights over it. Eight acres on the southern side of the close were assigned to the trustees of Rugby School. What was done with this land at first is not clear. The authorities of the school having exchanged 'the piece of land beyond the churchyard' (to which, if tradition be correct, the churchyard itself was sometimes annexed for purposes of play) for so large a play-ground, did not even feel it necessary, till 1816, to finish levelling the old Grange. In later times we find the new land in the occupation of the headmaster as a dairy farm, and finally in Dr. Goulburn's time (1850-57) it was incorporated in the close. The present New or Cricket Bigside was made out of it, while its outskirts afforded space in the course of years for the erection of racquet courts, gymnasium, and swimming bath.

Another Etonian, a Fellow of King's College, succeeded to Dr. James. This was Dr. Ingles, headmaster from 1794 to 1807, whom Dr. Wooll followed. It is curious to note that he and all the headmasters appointed in the present century have been Oxford men. Once more, in Dr. Wooll's time, the builders were busy. The old manor house and all the schools and barns attached to it came down piece by piece, and in their place arose the present school-house and old quadrangle. Six years were occupied in the erection of these buildings, at an expense of £32,000, from the plans, first of Mr. Samuel Wyatt, and, after his death, of Mr. Henry Hakewill, architect. A contemporary account in Ackermann's *History of Rugby School* describes these buildings with a touch of enthusiasm which may excuse its reproduction, instead of a more restrained description of them in comparison with modern developments and modern ideas as to the needs of schools. 'In about six years the present noble

Entrance to Headmaster's House

and extensive edifice was nearly finished, and appropriated to its intended purposes. It contains, or will contain (for the plan is not yet quite finished), everything that can be necessary for the convenience of those for whose occupancy it was intended. The headmaster's lodgings form a very handsome house; the grand entrance to them is very generally admired. With this house communicate several high and spacious apartments, formed over some of the schools, to be used as dormitories for those young gentlemen who form the headmaster's family. These rooms contain more than fifty beds, as every youth has his own bed, except in the instance of brothers of a certain age. A room is provided for the sick, fitted up with baths and everything necessary for such occasions. A large kitchen has a convenient connection with the dining-hall, but at a sufficient distance not to incommode that or any other part of the house. In the passage between the kitchen and dining-hall a communication is formed, chiefly by a staircase, with a pile of small apartments, forty in number, used as studies by the inmates of the house. In this part of the building a very proper attention seems to have been paid to the possible danger of fire, by a brick arch forming the roof of each story. A kind of arched gallery occupies the centre in each row, into which the doors of the studies open on each side; in each of these spaces there is a fireplace. No less than six spacious and lofty rooms are fitted up as schools; the largest of these is sixty-three feet six inches long, twenty-nine feet nine inches wide, and twenty-six feet high; all the others are of very handsome dimensions. In addition to these, a smaller room up-stairs is used for the same purpose, the approach to which is by a staircase in the north-west tower, and by a gallery formed over the east end of the most western school. In this room and gallery are temporary book-cases, erected for the books collecting for the future library. The entrance to the schools from the town is by a gateway with a pointed arch. Provision is made, by a tower for a staircase, for building a library over this gateway.[1] It leads into the quadrangle, the west side of which is

formed by the great school, and by the side of this a portico is intended to be built,[2] similar to those already finished on the east and south sides of this court. The

[1] This library, the old Sixth School, round which cluster vivid memories of Arnold in the hearts of his pupils, was added shortly after Arnold's appointment to the headmastership.

[2] This intention was never carried out.

door-way leading into the play-ground is at the west end of the south portico.'

Such were the buildings to which Arnold came in 1828, and which have been made famous as the scene of the youthful life and doings of Tom Brown, Pater Brooke, Flashman, and the other types of school character portrayed by the masterly hand of 'an old Boy.' In 1816 there were three or four boarding-houses kept by masters, others under the charge of various persons more or less connected with the school. In these buildings 381 boys (including town boys) were accommodated ; in these seven rooms, including the old big school, then known as the great school, this large number was somehow or other taught. Dr. Wooll was assisted by seven under-masters and two assistant-tutors. The account above referred to claims it as a particular excellence in this school, that each form had its own master, who attended to it, and no other. A busy time they must some of them have had ; in the school list of 1816 one form contains the names of fifty-nine boys, others are nearly as large.

Whosoever takes any interest in schools and their life has read and re-read the *Life of Arnold.* Amid all the interest of his many-sided mind, and of the masterly touch with which he treats of innumerable subjects of the highest moment in his letters, it may safely be said that the reader turns with deepest attention to the chapter headed 'School Life at Rugby.' The peculiar greatness of Arnold lay in the fact that he combined the two chief excellences of a teacher. Some men have been peculiarly great as trainers of intellect, some for their influence on character; some have combined the two powers. And pre-eminent among these was Arnold. From his time, indeed, dates the prominence of the idea, so familiar now, that school has something more important to do than to impart a certain amount of knowledge; it has to train character. Arnold never tired of impressing this upon his pupils; if the prophecy of Provost Hawkins in his testimonial, that Arnold, if elected, would change the face of education all through the public schools of England has in any way been verified, it is in this point. And more than any words of his could do, was done by the contact with the man himself, as boys began to know him. There was a 'sympathetic thrill, caught from a spirit that was earnestly at work in the world,' from the conviction of his intense abhorrence of moral evil, from the evidence of his own life that he regarded life as a whole in which all true manliness must be based on the practical exercise of the highest principles, that fired the spirit of his colleagues and pupils and friends. So it came to pass that the ideal arose, not of a perfect society in which there should be no black spots, but of one in which old and young should be, in their sphere, working together for good. 'What I have often said before' (he said to the sixth), 'I repeat now; what we must look for here is, first, religious and moral principle; secondly, gentlemanly conduct; thirdly, intellectual ability.' Readers of the lately published life of Archbishop Tait will remember the graphic account of the speech which he made on his last day at Rugby, and the noble words in which he reiterated this teaching.

Of course there was much else for Arnold to do. The range of subjects of education was narrow. History, Modern Languages, Mathematics had to be gradually introduced into the regular curriculum ; the system of boarding-houses had to be remodelled, a hundred points to be in their turn attended to. The great fame of Arnold was reared, not upon his mastery of these details, but upon the great principles to which he gave life and reality, and which in later years have borne fruit in the difference between the public schools of our time and the places of which Cowper and others wrote a century ago.

On the sudden death of Arnold, in June 1842, his Rugby friends were sorely exercised as to the question of his successor. Some of their expressions of feeling may seem exaggerated ; indeed, in recent years, it has been in some quarters not uncommon to represent the work and influence of Arnold as having been over-rated by his earliest admirers. It is more probable that this feeling is due to the difficulty of realising the facts of his work ; many of the ideas and principles into which his vigorous spirit breathed life, seem now-a-days so axiomatic, so obvious, so natural a part of our mental and moral furniture, that it is hard to believe that they would have seemed so alien to men of the first decades of this century. Ten days after Arnold's death the name of Archibald Campbell Tait was on the list of candidates for the office. An interesting anecdote is recorded in his recently published *Life*, which testifies to the feeling aroused by Arnold's death. Tait was paying a visit in Northamptonshire. 'The visit over (writes Lady Wake) Archie returned to Oxford. I had gone with him to Blisworth Station to see him off, when our attention was attracted by the sight of a multitude of boys filling the carriages of the train, all silent and sad. "Who were they?" "The young gentlemen from Rugby," was the reply. Evidently it was no holiday. "What brought them there?" "Arnold is dead," passed from mouth to mouth. Their hushed voices and subdued looks told evidently how suddenly the blow had fallen, and how it had affected each one of them.' Amid a number of distinguished candidates, some of Arnold's best-known pupils encouraged him to stand, but it was with fear and trembling. Dean Lake wrote to him, 'O, my dear Tait, I do not envy you if you do get it. I quite quake for the awful responsibility, putting on that giant's armour.' Stanley wrote in a similar strain, speaking a few weeks later of 'the awful intelligence' of his election.

Tait was elected, and there followed some seven years of quiet, unobtrusive work. It was a difficult position; it was necessary not only to keep up the Arnold ideals; 'there was truth as well as humour in his remark,' writes Dean Bradley, 'that we had other things to do at Rugby besides exalting the Arnold tradition.' These other things consisted not only in hard business work, in ordering and regulating much that was difficult to arrange owing to the great influx of boys to the school. Every new movement, however good it is, is attended by its own dangers and possibilities of excess. Arnold's sixth-form system was liable to produce at times an unnatural and excessive, because premature, development of the character, and to render the relations of the sixth with their authority almost hostile to the school at large. Tait had to work the system so as to check the evil without endangering the good. 'To the Rugby of that day,' writes one of his old pupils, 'a little cold water from time to time, kindly administered, was not without its uses.' Tait was successful in his task, not only by positive regulations and exhortation, but still more perhaps by the use of the quiet humour which was natural to him, and of which very characteristic specimens dot the few pages allotted in his life to the Rugby career of the future archbishop.

A severe illness in 1848 brought out striking expression of the warm feeling which his quiet, gentle rule had generated, and of which many of his Rugby friends and pupils were, up to that time, half unconscious themselves. It is indeed thought by some still living, who remember him at Rugby, that the biography scarcely does justice to the success of his headmastership, and especially to the deep and genuine influence which he exercised, not only in the school, but in the town, and on all who had to do with him.

After the lapse of a few more quiet years under the rule of Dr. Goulburn, afterwards Dean of Norwich till 1889, the chief came to the school, who has been the most famous of its headmasters, after Arnold, in the present century. This was Dr. Temple, the present Bishop of London, who governed Rugby from 1858 till his appointment to the Bishopric of Exeter in 1869. It was fortunate that the tercentenary of the foundation of the worthy grocer came at a time when the school was at the height of prosperity and success. A very large sum of money was raised, and in the course of years expended on the extension of the buildings of the school. So there rose up the enlarged chapel (of which more below), the new quadrangle, gymnasium, and racquet courts, the observatory, the Temple Library and Art Museum. Naturally the erection of these buildings took many years. The process was carried on during Dr. Hayman's mastership, and was pushed forward vigorously by Dr. Jex Blake, who succeeded to him. The generous example which Dr. Jex Blake himself set by the gift to the school of a swimming bath (with the inscription over the door 'Rugbeiensibus Rugbeiensis'), elicited new generosity on the part of other old Rugbeians. The new big school, with form rooms underneath, was built, and finally the school premises were enlarged by the purchase of a second playing field, Caldecott Piece.

Of the architectural style of the buildings erected since the tercentenary, it may be as well to say little. Their beauty is a somewhat disputed question; the outlines of some of them are somewhat original, and the colouring afforded by the lavish use of bricks of various hues is vivid. A sketch of the history of the school may be excused for avoiding controversy. It may suffice to say that, in her buildings as a whole, Rugby possesses a very ample provision for the needs of a large school. But, alas! for the word 'finally' used a few lines back. In schools there is no finality; what one generation prides itself on as more than usually complete, the next generation finds insufficient. Already the cry is making itself heard for new homes for the teaching of science; and by the time they can be provided, no doubt new buildings will be needed for something else.

When Arnold came to Rugby, the chapel, with which his memory is so closely connected, had been in existence some eight years. It was in some ways a remarkable building. No less an authority than Mr. M. H. Bloxam was of opinion that, though not without its faults, the old chapel was in advance of its age. But it was not a very advanced age in the revival of Gothic architecture. Internally the chapel presented 'the beautiful proportions of three cubes,' being ninety feet long by thirty feet high and thirty in breadth, and having a flat ceiling. Solidly and firmly built, it was decorated externally with twelve ponderous buttresses, which must have been regarded as ornamental. Consecrated in 1820 in the name of St. Lawrence, this chapel was the subject of constant alteration; at the present time, nothing remains of it except a portion of the west end, to which the main body of the present chapel has been built on, and windows and monuments transferred from the one to the other. Dr. Arnold's letters contain reference to 'his old enemy the flat roof,' and to his plans for getting rid of it. This was not effected till 1852.

In 1845 and subsequent years transepts were thrown out, a new porch built at the west end, the old buttresses robbed of their massive magnitude, and various other smaller improvements made. In later years the whole building, with the exception, as has been said, of the western portion, was removed, and the present chapel was erected from the design of Mr. Butterfield.

Owing to these constant changes, though at school generation follows rapidly after generation, the bricks and mortar of the chapel have not yet acquired for Rugbeians the charm of age, and of the memories which age brings. To the non-Rugbeian visitor the chapel will present a study not devoid of interest in the bold outlines of the building, and the ingenuity with which the architect has united new and old, and has given to the east end an air of dignity, which it was difficult to get in the narrow limits available, even if the final opinion should be adverse to it on account of the want of restfulness in the colouring, and the lack of gracefulness in the lines of the exterior and in the proportions of the interior. Yet is it the first place to which the visitor turns, and the one which becomes the most inspiring memory of most Rugby boys. In spite of change and shifting, that pulpit is the pulpit of Arnold and of Temple; the plain grey stone just at the foot of the chancel steps marks the spot where Arnold's body was laid under the communion-table of the old chapel; the glorious east window is one of the four windows of ancient stained glass, which, mainly through Arnold's own exertions, were procured on the Continent for the chapel; the little chair and table in the vestry are those which he used in the old sixth school; the monument on the wall in the north transept is both the memorial of his great friendship with Bunsen, who composed the inscription, and the record of his character and work. Fitly, after enumerating some of his titles to fame, does it imply that his greatest work was his school work at Rugby, and his chief memorial in the life of those whom he taught

IUVENUM ANIMOS MONUMENTUM SIBI DELIGENS.

ASHBY ST. LEGERS

GUNPOWDER PLOT

ONE of the many rural and pleasant parts of England is Ashby St. Legers. It may be reached easily through Hillmorton and Kilsby; very delightful indeed the walk is, and some two hours would accomplish it, but there are stations at Crick and Kilsby that land us within easy distance. Kilsby church is of no great interest, and it was modernised in 1869; but the long tunnel between it and Crick is a sort of national monument as far as railways are concerned. This tunnel is one and three-quarter miles in length, and is ventilated by two large shafts, twenty yards across, and they average 100 feet in depth. There is an extensive quicksand that almost runs with the tunnel, and caused some danger in the construction of the underway. The church of Ashby St. Legers is very interesting and beautiful; it is one of the very few churches in all England that have not been wrecked inside and modernised with light rush-bottom chairs or deal benches, to the great sorrow of those whose forefathers sat in the old oak pews. Mr. Senhouse is the lord of the manor, and he has, to the great satisfaction of the preservers of the ancient buildings of England, refused any demolition of the old oak-work, and the church is

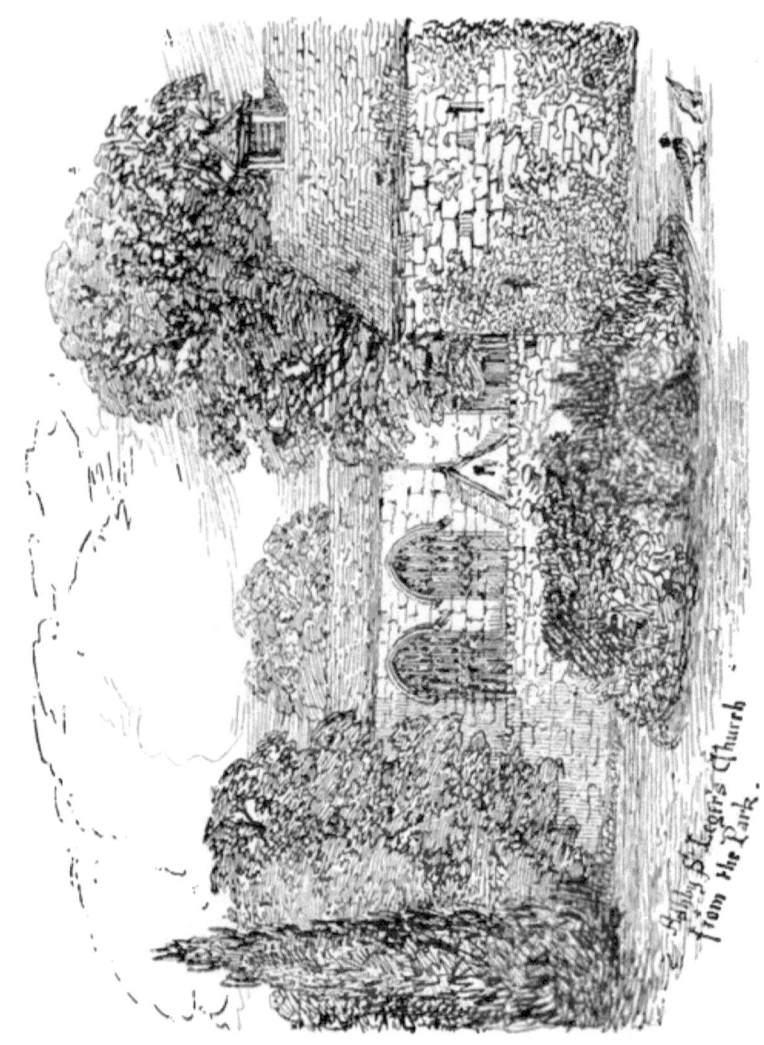
Ashby St. Leger's Church from the Park.

as it was, and indeed as so many churches in the kingdom ought to be. There is no clerestory to the church, but there is a fine arcade, and all the church may be said to date back to the fifteenth century. The Rood screen with canopied top is in good condition, and the staircase projects into the south aisle. The tower seems earlier than the rest of the church, since the nave aisles are built up against it. In the glass of one of the windows was Sir John de Catesby and his wife. He died in 1437, and he was the grandfather of Sir William Catesby, whose name is, through Shakespeare, so immortally connected with history. Many are the records of him, and he was the one alluded to by a fancy poet that lost his life through his erratic verse on Richard, whose crest was a blue boar, and his followers—

'The cat, the rat, and Lovell the dog,
Do rule all England under a hog.'

Some relics of these followers still remain in England, and indeed they are precious. Ashby, of course, is connected with the Catesbys. The Ratcliffes lived at Ordsall Hall, in Manchester, a noble building that still stands in all its beauty, though surrounded by small streets in every direction, and Lovell at Minster Lovell, near Oxford, an unfrequented scene; but as many Rugby scholars will go, in time, to Oxford, one cannot too strongly recommend them to pay it a visit. It is delightfully situated in the valley of the Windrush, and though it gives the idea of a gloomy old mansion, the details are delicate and very beautiful, so we may fairly say that we are indebted to the then followers of

Richard III. for relics of beauty. Minster Lovell is an admirable example of the time when, like Kenilworth, feudal castles were beginning to be converted into manor houses. But to return to Ashby, the gate-house, which is shown, and which is open to the public road, is extremely picturesque, and forms a delightful group with the ancient church. It is well worthy of a much longer pilgrimage than that from Rugby, and is an example of the black and white which does not, as a rule, prevail in this part of England, where building-stone was plentiful. We must go to Lancashire, and Cheshire, and counties that were densely crowded with heavy oak trees for wood and plaster work. Nothing, of course, can be more shocking and wicked than the gunpowder plot which was hatched, perhaps originally, in the gate-house shown, but a short history of it that does not appear always in school-books might go far to explain it.

Shakespeare, as is commonly the case, has given a true historical account of Wolsey and Cromwell, as indeed he has done in events that were more remote from his own days than they were. Luther and Catherine of Arragon may perhaps be considered as the causes of the destruction of monasteries in England, and, to use the words of Green in speaking of Wolsey, he says, 'Great as was Wolsey's pride, he regarded himself and proclaimed himself merely as the creature of the king. Henry had rewarded him munificently for his services to the crown. He had been raised to the see of Lincoln, and the Archbishopric of York;

the revenues of two other sees, whose tenants were foreigners, were in his hands; he was the Bishop of Winchester and Abbot of St. Albans; he was in receipt of pensions from France and Spain, while his official emoluments were enormous.' His state was quite royal, and his retainers consisted of 500 persons of noble birth. 'In raising his favourite to the head of the church and state, Henry was simply gathering all

Ashby St Legers Gunpowder plot house.

religious as well as civil authority into his personal grasp.' Wolsey was not worthy of his high state, and wished to govern without a Parliament, but the downfall is grandly told by Shakespeare, and his servant Cromwell was really his friend.

It was on the high measures he took to separate Henry from Catherine of Arragon that Wolsey broke from the nobles of England, who were Catholics, and

Buckingham went so far as to say that when Henry was no more Wolsey should go to the block, but Act 3 of Henry VIII. tells all in matchless language, and when Wolsey fell he said to Cromwell:

> 'Get thee from me, Cromwell.
> I am a poor fallen man, unworthy now
> To be thy lord and master. Seek the king.
> That sun I pray may never set! I have told him
> What and how true thou art.'

Cromwell's rule, as we know, was terrible to the Catholics, and it has been called the 'English reign of terror,' for Catholicism was the religion of the country, and, as has been said, words idly spoken, the murmurs of an abbot, or even the terrors of a nun, were converted into high treason, and the gibbet was brought into requisition. It is supposed that in the time of Henry VIII. nearly half of England belonged to the Catholic Church, but it was entirely transferred by Cromwell. The commission that was employed to look into the state of the monastic houses did not, it is true, give a very favourable account of all. Some were well conducted, but many of them had records that showed their way of life was not well, and I wish it lay out of my power to add that too many of the carvings in abbey or priory churches of the fifteenth century tend to confirm the record.

All the religious houses were dissolved, and the lands given to court favourites. Abbeys and priories were converted into dwellings, of which many remain to the present day in possession of the families to whom they were granted; and, what is the worst feature of all abbots, and priors, and monks were hung, sometimes even before their own abbey gates. Cromwell had indeed, gone so far as to sentence men without trial. We find in his papers such shocking items as these :— 'Item.—The Abbot of Reading to be sent down and executed at Reading.' 'Item.—When Master Fisher shall go to his execution, and the other.' He sent Sir Thomas More to the block because he would not agree to the king's supremacy over the church, though More was looked upon then, and even yet, as the foremost of Englishmen in intellect and character, and in everything that constitutes greatness.

Catholics were deprived of civil rights, and compelled to go to the reformed church, under heavy penalties. Men were even put to death in Elizabeth's time for their religious beliefs, though, happily, she stopped this. Still, when the clergy sent a petition in which they declared their loyalty to the crown, but begged that if they from conscience abstained from joining the Established Service they should be mercifully considered, they were rebuffed. Richard Shelly presented the petition, and he was committed to prison at once, where, after several years of solitude, he died. Now it is hardly to be wondered at that zealots, such as the Catholics, were beginning to hatch conspiracies. There were several in Elizabeth's time, such as the Babington, where Tichbourne was induced to come in, and a number were executed; but it was supposed by the Catholics that James I., from his parentage, would restore them to their old condition.

Robert Catesby, who was taken at Bosworth Field was, after the battle, executed. It was to him that Richard called out at the end of the battle :

A horse ! a horse ! my kingdom for a horse !

His estates were attainted ; but afterwards they were restored into the possession of the family.

At the period of the Gunpowder Plot, Lady Catesby lived at Ashby St. Legers. Her son, who afterwards figured so remarkably in our records, is spoken of as a fine, noble-looking man, more than six feet in height, and having a fine open countenance. He married a daughter of Sir Thomas Leigh, of Stoneleigh ; a beautiful abbey it was, dedicated to the Cistercian order, and delightfully situated. Catesby, so far as we can know from State papers, first devised the plot, though doubtless there are others, whose names will never appear, that were in concert with him. We hear of Winter, a country gentleman from Huddington, in Worcester, who was his early coadjutor, and he was a known conspirator, having been connected with all the plots in Elizabeth's time. Indeed, so far had he conspired that he actually went over to Spain to induce the King to send the Armada to attack England. Guy Fawkes belonged to a respectable Yorkshire family, and of course his name is, though not quite justly, the one most connected with the plot. Percy, who was one of the early additions to the conspiracy, was in some way connected with the House of Northumberland. He was a gentleman pensioner, and had certain duties that he should perform in Parliament, and, taking advantage of this, he rented the residence next to the Houses of Parliament as his town abode. John Wright, who was also a landed proprietor, joined the band, and they occupied Percy's town residence with great secrecy. But the State trials have given a very lucid and clear account of the whole proceedings. They worked an underground passage to the Parliament House, and came to the walls of the building itself. These were, it is needless to say, powerfully and well built with the best of stones and mortar; they were nine feet in thickness, and this brought them, after some hard work, to despair. Then they decided to enlist other workers, and make them take the solemn oath, and they found one, Mr. Keyes, of Lambeth, and John Wright's brother, suitable and reliable comrades. It appeared in the evidence that they were afraid of being seen as occupying the same town house. They were Catholics of standing, and, as Fawkes said at the trial, the walls were attacked for days, not by workmen, but by gentlemen of rank. There was a garden-house on one side of the dwelling and a small garden, and here each night they took the soil they had excavated from the passage, scattering it early in the morning over the grass, raking it flat and covering it with turf which was kept for the purpose. They did not go out more than one at a time, and Catesby laid in a stock of eggs, baked meat, and biscuits. Catesby knew that if he did succeed in his scheme there would still be some trouble and risings among the Protestants to put down, and he, in consequence, collected a large quantity of arms, and had them kept at Ashby St. Legers. This he did openly, as he affirmed that he was going to send troops to Flanders at his own charge. He now secured the services of Sir Everard Digby, the head of the Digby family, who were settled at Stoke Dry. Gough, in speaking of him, says that he was one of the 'handsomest men and the finest gentleman of his time.' There is a

Digby Monument, Stoke Dry.

monument in the chancel to his ancestor Kenelm Digby, and his wife. It is finely carved in alabaster, which bears the date of 1590, and round the sides are figures in the high Elizabethan frills. Parliament was prorogued from February 7th to October 3rd, and then again to November 5th; and it was then, when King James would be there, that the terrible crime was proposed to be committed. There was one singular event that they say occurred during the breaking down of the wall when they were in the middle of their work. The State trial records that they heard a bell tolling, and looked at each other terror-stricken. At last they threw some holy water on the ground, and the sound ceased. Another sound, however, occurred, which gave them great fright, and that was a heavy noise overhead. They supposed they were discovered, but found out afterwards that it was one, Bright, who had a stock of fuel, and was removing it for sale. Guy Fawkes at once saw how superior this place would be for their purpose, and the cellar was hired. Many barrels of gunpowder were conveyed from Lambeth at night, and crow-bars and other tools were concealed among them, and these were again covered up with fagots and other things to prevent their being seen. Now, some of the conspirators had relatives in the House of Lords, and they urged Catesby to advise them to be absent, but he utterly refused, and said that 'rather than that the project should not take place, if they were as dear to me as my own son they must be blown up,' though he said he hoped that most of the Catholics would be absent, so as not to have to deal with laws which made their religion penal. Now Tresham, one of the conspirators, had two Catholic brothers-in-law in the Upper House, Lord Monteagle and Lord Stourton, and he wrote a letter to Monteagle, which has been often reproduced, begging him not to venture to come to the House on the 5th of

November, as a danger threatened Parliament, and they should not even see who hurt them. Monteagle happened to be away at his house at Hoxton, and he was sitting down to supper when his page brought in the letter. It is said that when he saw the letter contained neither signature nor date he treated it very cavalierly, and threw it to a gentleman who was sitting down in the room, and after a short time he advised Lord Monteagle that there was probably something of more import than he was aware of in the matter, and it is more than probable that he had some vague idea of what was impending. It was suspected by Catesby and Winter that Tresham had revealed the plot to Monteagle, for Monteagle's valet told Thomas Winter about the letter, and they summoned him to attend them—a summons that he promptly obeyed—and the fact of his having been absent for some few days quite confirmed their suspicion. They accused him when he came of writing the letter, and they had their rapiers ready to run him through to the heart, but he so absolutely denied every knowledge of it that they put up their swords in their sheaths, though they gravely doubted the truth of his denials. His courage was certainly great to submit to the ordeal. How far Monteagle was advised of the circumstances of the case we can never know, but it does seem a little strange that he should have gone with the Lord Chamberlain of London to look round the building, and under the floors of the house. They went down to the cellars, and actually saw Guy Fawkes some time before the 5th of November, and he told them he was merely a servant of Percy's; but they were struck with the great quantity of coal and firewood that the cellar contained. It is out of all reason to suppose that James I. had any hand in discovering the object of the letter, and the terrible warning it contained, though he certainly claimed as much for himself, and some English histories have even adopted his version of the case. The letter itself ran as follows :—

'MY LORD,—Out of the love that I bear to some of your friends I have a care of your preservation; therefore I advise you, as you tender your life, to devise some excuse to shift off your attendance at this Parliament, for God and man have concurred to punish the wickedness of this time; and think not lightly of this advertisement, but retire yourself into your country, where you may expect the event in safety: for though there is no appearance of any stir, yet I say they will receive a terrible blow this Parliament, and yet they shall not see who hurts them. This counsel is not to be contemned, because it may do you good, and can do you no harm, for the danger is passed as soon as you have burned the letter. And I hope God will give you grace to make good use of it, to Whose holy protection I commend you.'

There is every appearance in the letter itself that it came from a relation who was himself one of the conspirators, and every circumstance would point out Tresham as the author, notwithstanding his denial. After the visit of Monteagle and the Chamberlain to the cellars, Sir Thomas Knevet went down, and there he found Fawkes with the slow matches, and his capture is too well known to repeat. There is a strong probability that Monteagle himself knew more of the circumstances of the plot than is commonly accredited to him, and the fact of letting it remain so long unfettered was to enable the conspirators to escape. Fawkes was taken before the King and Council, and in reply to the question of how he could possibly have the cruelty to destroy so many persons of innocence, he said, 'Dangerous diseases need desperate remedies.' To one of James' Scottish courtiers, who asked him why so many barrels of gunpowder were brought together, he replied, 'to blow Scotchmen back to Scotland.' His self-possession never gave way during the examination. And when he was asked to divulge the names of the real conspirators, for he was hardly more than a servant, he utterly refused, and when he was told that was useless, as their flight made them known, he said in reply that it would be superfluous for him to divulge the names if they had divulged themselves, and he added that he was willing to die himself, but he would rather die ten thousand deaths than betray his friends. Over what happened in the next two days in the torture chambers we willingly draw a veil.

ASHBY ST. LEGERS
AND THE SENHOUSE FAMILY

ASHBY ST. LEGERS is a charming residence. Much of the ancient architecture remains. The end shown is very admirable in design and proportion, and has not been altered. Here it was that one of the most dramatic events in the whole of the plot occurred. The hall itself will be shortly noticed afterwards. Catesby and John Wright, supposing that success was bound to attend the efforts of Guy Fawkes, rode off to Dunchurch to join the gathering band of Catholics for which arms had been provided. It is not to be supposed that they were joint conspirators, but it was thought that when the king and the Protestant representatives of the people (for a Catholic could not sit in the House) were blown up by gunpowder, a sudden rising would take place, which would be led by the conspirators, and the Princess Elizabeth placed on the throne. Christopher and John Wright followed.

Now Rookwood and Keyes were but little known in London, though, of course, the features of the principal conspirators were, and they stayed behind to report the success of the plot and transfer its news to Catesby and his associates. They noticed on the 6th November that when they ventured out there were small groups talking in horror at the latest news, and saw at once that their cause was over. Keyes, who was the better known of the two, fled away at once, but Rookwood remained in the city till noon, when he also went away to join Catesby at Ashby St. Legers. He overtook Keyes on the road, who parted from him, and then he went at a rapid pace till he overtook Catesby and John Wright. He told them of their utter reverse, and they all pushed on till they overtook Percy and Christopher Wright, riding on as fast as the fleetest horses could carry them till they reached their destination at Ashby St. Legers. Now Sir Everard Digby had gone to Dunchurch on the 5th November to collect his forces in order to back up the plot after the king and his government were killed, and in order to obtain the latest particulars he went to Ashby St. Legers to visit Lady Catesby. There were a number of Catholics there who were just on the point of sitting down to supper, quite believing that the plot could not fail, when the five fugitives rushed in, broken down with fatigue, and told their news. Great as the dismay was, it did not stop their projected revolt, and they still hoped. So infatuated had they become, in hopes the Catholics would rise, that when they heard of the capture of Fawkes they still believed the sword would gain their ends, and they quite refused to put it up in its sheath.

When Sir Everard's guests at Dunchurch had heard of the complete failure of the plot, they quietly stole away, leaving no trace they could avoid behind them. But the infatuated conspirators had for long so worked themselves up to a hopeless cause that they still continued their revolt, and believed that at last England would join them; and they went away to Holbeach, a place on the borders of Staffordshire, where one Stephen Littleton lived. And now all hope was cut off. Not one man, as Sir Everard Digby did, came to help them, though they all expected a great multitude, and then they began to lose all their courage. Many of them, as the record says, perceiving God to be against them, prayed before a picture of Our Lady, and confessed that the act was so bloody that they desired God to forgive them. But all was over, and they knew it; Sir Richard Walsh was high sheriff of the county at the time, and he soon had collected a *posse comitatus* that was sufficient to crush the conspirators. Holbeach was surrounded and fired into, and while Thomas Winter was crossing the yard his arm was broken by a shot. 'Stand by me,' Catesby said, 'and we will die together.' And so it indeed turned out, for soon after they were both, happily for themselves, pierced by musket balls, and John and Christopher Wright were fortunate enough to meet the same end, as also was Percy; but he was the last of them, and all the rest of the conspirators were taken prisoners.

They were executed at the west end of St. Paul's. But there is one single exception to the list of the public executions, and that is Tresham's. He died the day before his trial in the Tower, and this brings a decided suspicion that his former divulgences may most probably have secured him some drug from the powers that were.

Ashby St Legers

And so his shocking doom (for shocking their ways of leaving life then were) might be toned down. But it is very probable that, though they did not know it, the introduction of Jesuits into England that had just occurred had some connection with the plot. Garnett was their leader, and at his trial Chief Justice Coke spoke of him as 'by birth a gentleman, by education a scholar, by art learned, and a good linguist.'

Tulip Tree, Ashby St. Legers.

Though the part shown of Ashby St. Legers is old, and there are many remains of antiquity that are carefully preserved, the garden-front of the hall is modern, but built in keeping with the rest, and the whole group with its gables, and oriels, and ivy-clothing is very charming. The billiard-room, with its wainscot, is an ancient apartment, and is supposed to have been originally the chamber where Lady Catesby and her friends were sitting down to supper when the conspirators rushed in with the news from London. The park at Ashby St. Legers can be seen from the road very well, and there is a pathway through a beautiful part of it. It contains a picturesque lake, and is well wooded. Amongst its trees is a tulip tree which is supposed to be the largest in England.

These trees are uncommon, and are only seen in extensive grounds, but they are very beautiful, and the tulip flower looks strangely out of place on such a tree. They do not flower every year, but their flowering is early in the season, and they are also very shapely. There is also here a cedar of Lebanon that is of noble proportions, and any one who at all links its growth with the yew-tree in age would be surprised to hear that it is not seventy years old, though another cipher would be required to be added to the seventy to make it equal in age to yews that it certainly resembles in magnitude and appearance. The late proprietor of Ashby St. Legers would, I am told, allow no trees to be cut down, until at last they became almost too dense, and the present owner very wisely decided to thin them a little, and give the others, which still form a well-wooded, or almost densely-wooded estate, a little more open space. Catesby was, of course, attainted, and his lands, which were escheated to the Crown, were granted to Sir William Irwing. In the year 1612, Ashby St. Legers was purchased from the Irwing family, and it remained in their possession for ninety-one years, when it was sold to Joseph Ashley, whose present family representative is the successor to the property. Mr. Pocklington Senhouse is the present owner.

The family of Senhouse dates to Richard I.'s time, and many are the scenes in English records with which their names are connected. But two may be mentioned. John Senhouse, in 1599, entertained the celebrated antiquary Camden, and is mentioned by Camden in his *Britannia* as having collected with great industry many Roman stones, altars, lavers, and statues with inscriptions, which he had with much judgment placed in his houses and buildings. Richard Senhouse was fellow of St. John's, Cambridge. When a scholar at Cambridge he went to Cumberland to see his friends, and as his horse happened to cast a shoe he went to a smith's to have it shod, but found he had left his purse behind. The smith said, 'Well, well, never mind, you will pay me when you come to be Bishop of Carlisle.' He did become Bishop of Carlisle in 1624, and abundantly he repaid the blacksmith when reminded of the promise. He preached the coronation sermon before Charles I. Mr. Humphrey Senhouse it was who founded the harbour of Maryport, in Cumberland, which he called after the christian name of his wife, and which is now becoming so valuable a property.

There is one word to add about Sir Everard Digby before leaving the plot and its associations, and the fine old church of Stoke Dry, where the family remains lie, all quite within reach of Rugby, and seated in a charming country. Sir Everard had conveyed this and many other manors to himself for life, and to his heir-in-tail on his demise; but on his execution for his part in the shocking crime his manors and estates were claimed for the Crown. Had this plea been made a little later on, in the days when Jeffreys, and Wright, and Scroggs have left so immortal a record in the memorials of the Stuarts, of course it would not have been even disputed; but the judges who tried it were incorrupt, and the two chief judges and the chief baron decided that under the will of Sir Everard Digby he was only a tenant for life, and his son Kenelm was in the light of a purchaser. 'The Crown could not have the special wardship, but only when there was an heir-general or special; whilst in this case there was not, the blood being corrupted, and the said Kenelm, having no heritable blood in him from his father, neither was he special heir-in-tail by form of the statute of Westminster, but came to the estate as a mere purchaser.'

CRICK CHURCH AND NEIGHBOURHOOD

If, on a visit to this charming county, it is decided to return by rail, Crick Station is near. Crick contains a church of great architectural interest. The spire, which is shown, is what is called a chamfered spire, in distinction from a broached one, the latter term being

applied to those spires that blend from the square tower to the octagon upper structure through a wedge-like triangle. In Crick the square tower dies into the octagonal spire, which belongs to the comparatively early decorated period. Crick is a contraction

Crick Church.

of Cerrig, which is a stone, or a rock, or crag, and doubtless it derived its name from the hilly country about it. Part of the church is early English, and was built probably in the early part of Henry III.'s reign; but the chancel, which is a deep one, is an excellent example of late decorated work, probably dating to the time of Edward III. The chancel arch is wide and lofty, and it springs from brackets with the heads of a king and a bishop. The sedilia and the piscina are well worthy of examination; the sedilia especially are very rich. The font is a cylinder, and is supported by three dwarfs.

Half a mile beyond Crick the high road crosses the old line of Watling Street, which is here visible for a considerable distance in each direction. Crick is the turning-point of the famous 'Crick run' of the boys at Rugby School. Close to Crick Station is Watford. The church is interesting, and well worthy of a visit. The chancel is of unusual length in comparison to the church. It is lit by three perpendicular windows on the south side, and on the north there is an archway, now blocked up, which led to a chantry that has been converted into a vestry. There are some well-carved tomb recesses in the chancel, of which it would seem that no record remains.

Close to the church is Watford Court, a beautiful manor house of the Elizabethan period, and the park is surrounded by a neatly trimmed hedge. Watford Manor is the seat of Lord Northington, who is a son-in-law of Sir Robert Peel. The first Lord Henley was a distinguished diplomatist, and made an excellent record all over Europe. He was raised to the Irish peerage in 1799, and the family to the English in 1885. The pleasant seat, Ashby Lodge, is near, and not far from the Warwickshire border, and nothing can be more delightful for a ramble than the lanes about here. Wild-flowers, birds, and butterflies abound here in the summer-time, and the road through Braunston Cleves, which leads to the ridge, is worthy of a long pilgrimage. Perhaps the most interesting feature in this district is that it is the backbone of England. There are backbones, of course, in other parts of the kingdom, but this is the great one, and it extends from the Dorsetshire coast to the Humber. Of course a backbone is a watershed, and rivers running in different directions on each side. 'The rocks that compose Northamptonshire are in age and character midway between those older beds that lie to the west, forming the coal-fields of Warwickshire, etc., and the newer chalk deposits which occur to the east. The strata run in long bands of varying width from north-east to south-west, coinciding almost exactly with the longest axis of the county, which is much elongated in this direction. The dip or slant of the rock-masses is towards the south-east, so that they overlie each other in this direction. Thus if we were to make a very deep boring, say at Stony Stratford or Peterborough, we should find at a considerable depth the same blue clays (lias) which occupy the surface on the west, near Market Harborough and Rugby.'

While on the subject of the Catesbys we might refer to the older branch of the family that figures in Richard III. The battle of Bosworth Field was fought on a great common that is not much altered, and it is well worthy of a visit. Bosworth lies a little to the west of the middle of Leicestershire, and is some miles from any railway station. Atherstone is probably the most convenient, and its name figures much in the battle. There can be no doubt that Shakespeare's very graphic account of Bosworth is the best. Some of his ancestral relatives were there, and in his days legends and verbal records were of value historically. In the fifth act King Richard says, after his sudden and seemingly nervous dialogue with Norfolk and Surrey the night before Bosworth field—

> Up with my tent. Here will I lie to-night ;
> But where to-morrow ? Well, all's one for that.
> Who hath descried the number of the traitors ?
>
> *Norfolk.*—Six or seven thousand is their utmost power.
>
> *King Rich.*—Why our battalia trebles that account.
> Besides, the King's name is a tower of strength,
> Which they upon the adverse faction want.
> Let us survey the vantage of the ground—
> Call for some men of sound direction :
> Let's want no discipline, make no delay ;
> For, lords, to-morrow is a busy day.

And busy it was. There is a correct account, so far as it can be traced, in Hutton, who says that his army, which consisted almost entirely of foot, was in two divisions, arranged in columns five abreast. The few horse that he had, formed the wings and kept near the centre. Hutton says that such a cavalcade would strike awe, because it would be fully an hour in leaving Nottingham, and quite an hour in marching through Leicester Gates. Richard rested that night at the Blue Boar Inn, called, possibly, by that name in after times from the animal on his armorial bearings. It is said also that here his body was brought after the battle, and buried in a stone coffin, which was afterwards used as a drinking trough for the farmers' horses. Richard left

Blue Boar Tavern

Leicester on the 17th, and on the 18th, he went to Stapleton, and encamped at a place called the 'Bradshaws.' But, finally, Richmond and Richard met on a marshy kind of plain, that has not really altered since the battle. It covers about 1500 acres. According to Shakespeare, Richard's army mustered some 20,000 men, and Richmond's was only about a third ; but the sudden change of front by Stanley and his forces to

Richmond made the balance very different, though still Richard was the stronger. He had, however, quite made up his mind that the day would be his. Lovell the Lord Chamberlain, Catesby the Attorney-General, and Sir Richard Radcliffe, all attended on the king, and to them he told the terrible dreams he had had before Bosworth Field. When he went from his tent early in the morning he saw a sentinel asleep and stabbed him, saying, 'I found him asleep, and left him as I found him.' He then commanded his troops to muster on Sutton Field, about the midway to Amyon Hill. Here he drew up his army in line of battle, and made his oration—

'Fight, gentlemen of England! fight, bold yeomen!
Draw, archers, draw your arrows to the head,' etc.

The place is still called 'Dickens' Nook.' I was, indeed, not a little surprised at the relics of names which Richard left behind him. Asking a countryman which was the way to King Richard's well, he said, 'You mean King Dick's,' and pointed out the well. The water rises to the surface, and it is a convenient drinking-place for cattle. There is a stone triangular cover over three sides, and the fourth is open; and over the well on a stone slab is carved the following inscription: 'Aqua ex hoc puteo hausta sitim sedavit. Richardus tertius, Rex Anglice, cum Henrico comite de Richmondia accerrime atque infensissime prœlians, et vita pariter, ac sceptro ante noctem cariturus. 11 Kal. Sep., A.D. mccccIxxxv.'

Of the real history of Stanley at the battle, Hutton

says that history and tradition are somewhat silent, 'but he marched and halted with Richard as if solely attached to the cause, still keeping a little to his left, for it was evidently his design to amuse his master to the last moment. Richmond sent an express to Lord Stanley requesting his assistance in forming his men, for he earnestly wished to have Stanley with him for fear of disappointment; but he returned for answer that the earl must form them himself; he would come at a convenient season. He afterwards, however, left his son's corps to the care of an officer, and privately assisted for a short time.' A slight glance at the battle field will show how completely the severance of Stanley and his forces from Richard's army decided the battle. They were on the left flank, and George Stanley was kept by Richard as a hostage; and when a messenger suddenly came to Richard's camp, he says :—

> 'What says Lord Stanley? Will he bring his power?
> *Messenger.*—My lord, he doth deny to come.
> *King Rich.*—Off, instantly, with his son George's head!
> *Norfolk.*—My lord, the enemy is past the marsh.
>   After the battle let George Stanley die.
>   *King Richard III.*, Act 5.

Richmond's front, for want of numbers, was spread out very thinly, so as to appear to greater advantage. It was commanded by John de Vere, Earl of Oxford, whose father and brother, twenty years before, perished on one scaffold, owing to their adherence to the House of Lancaster; the left wing was commanded by Sir John Savage, and the right by Sir Gilbert Talbot—

three very able officers, though Henry himself had no knowledge of the arts of war, nor did he at all desire to attain to them.

The two chiefs, Hutton says, rode through the ranks and made oratorical speeches to them; but, as he says, 'These speeches, like those in the House of Commons, perhaps meet the eye rather mended.' 'While Lord Stanley was forming, the king sent Sir Robert Brakenbury with this singular but dreadful message, "My lord, the king salutes you, and commands your immediate attendance with your bands, or, by ——, your son shall instantly die."' Lord Stanley seems to have given up his son for lost, but urged Sir Reginald Bray aside, and told him to post back to Richmond, and press him to advance with all speed against Richard's army; and, as Hutton in his admirable work says, 'This active measure was intended to employ Richard otherwise than in executions.' But the reply that Brackenbury brought caused Richard to order the immediate execution of Lord Stanley's son. 'But Lord Ferrers, of Chartley, a man of great honour and humanity, touched with compassion, ventured to remonstrate with the king.' He told him, according to the records that are left—and there seems to be much truth in them—that the son, whatever the father was, was free from any blame, and his execution would be sure to divert the father, whose course was not clear; but it would make him an enemy to the king and his cause.

The armies advanced towards each other, and it is said that some balls found in the garden of a farmer named Hewitt, came from Richard's artillery, but cannonading was then little understood, and not very hurtful. Archers were far more formidable than artillerymen. Arrows began the conflict, and soon the sword took their place. Old records say, and that probably with truth, that Richard's army was not enthusiastic in his cause, and quite the reverse was the case with Richmond's, who well knew that if Richard was successful 'the axe and the halter' would finish what the sword had begun. The army of Richmond was spread out to add importance to its size; but during the battle the Earl of Oxford ordered the men to close in round their standards, which shortened their length of front, and Richard at once prepared to outflank them, for he was a ready general; but just at that time Stanley's forces that had been drawn on the left flank of Richard's troops stopped the outflanking, and showed themselves in favour of Richmond, and this went very far to settle the strife. The battle had raged for an hour, but at half-past eleven no real advantage had been gained on either side. Only the front line of each army had been engaged, and they had not varied much in their position to each other; but fate declared in favour of Richmond, and Richard began his desperate charge, almost hoping to turn the battle; but his cause was lost, and he fell fighting furiously. His body was taken to Leicester, where it was interred in the Blue Boar, that has given the name to Blubber Lane, and Henry VII. was crowned on Bosworth Field. Short as the battle was, it was full of import for English history, and to quote what I once wrote before: 'From the time when Richard galloped out of his ranks to the time when he fell can only have been some fifteen minutes, but how full of import were they to England! The house of Plantagenet was extinguished, the baron's power reduced to a name, and the church, then more wealthy and powerful than either, might have heard its own knell in the Leicester chimes that rang in the coronation of the Tudors.'

EDGEHILL AND NASEBY.

AMONG the many historical records of Rugby we may place the two great battles that began and ended the civil war. They were fought within an easy reach of Rugby school. Edgehill was, of course, the opening one, and Naseby the one that, in some three years

Edge Hill

afterwards, settled the issue, and well worth a longer walk than would take us to them they are, with the pleasant lanes and shady trees, and the many churches of antiquity, and old houses that figure in all directions round them. Before the battle of Edgehill Charles apparently resolved on war; but he might, before raising as he did the Royal Standard at Nottingham, have thought of the result, even if successful, and ominous indeed were the tokens. When Henry IV. was in camp before Shrewsbury, he said to his son,—

> 'How bloodily the sun begins to peer
> Upon yon bosky hill! The day looks pale
> At his distemperature.'

And the prince replied,—

> 'The southern wind
> Doth play the trumpet to his purposes,
> And by his hollow whistling in the leaves,
> Foretells a tempest and a blustering day.'

But success was before him, and this widely differs from the ominous weather of Nottingham when Charles planted his standard. Clarendon, in his painstaking history, says: 'The *Standard* was erected about six of the clock in the evening of a very stormy and tempestuous day. The king himself with a small train rode to the top of castle hill; Varney, the Knight Marshal, who was standard-bearer, carrying the standard which was then erected in that place with little other ceremony than the sound of drums and trumpets. Melancholy men observed many ill presages about that time. There was not one regiment of foot yet brought thither, so that the trained bands which the sheriff had drawn together were all the strength the king had for his person and the guard of his standard. There appeared no conflux of men in obedience to the proclamation. The arms and ammunition were not yet come from York, and a general sadness covered the whole town. The standard was blown down the same night it had been set up, by a very strong and unruly wind, and could not be fixed up again in a day or two till the tempest was allayed. This was the melancholy state of the king's affairs when the standard was set up;' so says Clarendon.

The chief officer of Charles was Prince Rupert, a rash young soldier who did Charles some harm, and so encouraged his men in spoliations that he was called 'Prince Robber' among the people. Charles marched to Shrewsbury and collected a number of men, and went from there to Kenilworth; but he could not enter Coventry, as both Coventry and Warwick were guarded by Lord Brooke of Warwick Castle. He went on to Edgehill, and it is narrated that he saw a country squire, Mr. Shuckburgh, of Shuckburgh, hunting, and the king asked him how he could so enjoy himself when his king was about to fight for his crown and his dignity, which induced him to go among his tenantry and raise a company, with which he joined the king. Rupert took up his quarters at Wormleighton, which is about one and a half miles to the north-east of Fenny Compton, and was the residence of the Spencers, whose descendants now live at Althorpe. Spencer was a man of immense wealth, and had herds of nearly 20,000 sheep, though tradition says that he never quite reached the number, as disease always attacked his flocks before they quite reached that record. The troops of Essex had posted themselves on the plain, with the little town of Kineton in their rear. This place is well worthy of a visit. Camden derives the name from Kine town, supposing that it was a great headquarter for cattle; but Dugdale gives a different origin, and says that it 'was in possession of Edward the Confessor, and very likely other kings before those days,' and that its name merely means 'a town belonging to the king.' At the north-east end of the town was a castle where King John once resided, but I cannot find any trace of it now. The church formerly belonged to Kenilworth priory, but it has lost much of its original interest, as it was partly rebuilt in the year 1775.

The kennels of the Warwickshire hounds are situated at Lower Kineton, and cost over £4000 in their erection. Edgecott House is in a very picturesque and well-wooded park. The present residence was built in 1752, and in its site was a Tudor mansion of which some interesting drawings remain. Here Charles slept the night before the battle of Edgehill, as also did his two sons, Charles and James. They arrived on October 22, 1642, and the following morning at three o'clock they were roused up with the news that the Parliamentary army was close, and Charles might at once fight them if he felt so disposed. This message came from the impetuous Rupert, and orders were at once given to march on Edgehill, where Charles passed by cross-roads that can easily be traced. Charles breakfasted at Radway, and a hillock is pointed out as the place where he advanced with a 'prospect glass' to take a survey of the enemy. He soon joined his nephew, and they formed a line of battle along the brow of the hill; the right rested upon Bullet Hill, and the centre where the king was is now marked by a sham ruin, just above Radway village. Charles was encased in complete armour, and was his own commander-in-chief. The Earl of Lindsey was the general under him, and a very able veteran he was. His descendant, the eleventh earl, now lives at Uffington, near Stamford. He took exception, however, to the childish insolence of Prince Rupert, and placed himself at the head of his own regiment. There was one singular feature early in the battle,—the sudden defection of Sir Faithful Fortescue from the Parliamentary side; he had been engaged to raise troops in England and Ireland, which were to be employed in the king's service in the north of Ireland, and to this he had the consent of Parliament. The war broke out just as he was about to embark at Bristol, and he was ordered by Parliament to march across the country and join the army of Essex, but he supposed that his troops were king's troops, and on finding his mistake he crossed to join Rupert. This completely confused the Parliamentarians, and enabled Rupert to succeed in his charge upon them; he completely routed them, and pursued them with great slaughter as far as Kineton. With the approval, however, of Rupert, and with his assistance, his detachment stopped for an hour to plunder the baggage of Essex's troops, and this materially altered the issue of the battle.

There is a place near Kineton called 'Rupert's

Headland,' and he managed to draw up his cavalry here when he heard that the Parliamentarians were again forming; but he was just too late, for Hampden, who was only a few marches in the rear, came up at this juncture, and opened fire. Rupert fell back quite routed, and the battle was raging round King Charles. His position was admirably chosen. 'Difficult ground in the right and left protected his flanks. Immediately in front the ridge of Edgehill, which stretches almost north and south, sinks suddenly down on what is called the 'central plain' of England, whilst at the northern end this ridge is crossed at a right angle by the Dassett Hills, which throw out a spur of high ground into the level. The king could thus overlook the entire position of his adversaries, which lay below him as on a map. So strong was his position that, if he had awaited the attack of Essex, he might have been certain of success; but the impetuous Rupert and other officers pushed on to meet the attack half way, and that was against the urgent advice of Lord Lindsey, who was a veteran and tried soldier. Charles was in full armour with the Garter Cross on his breastplate; but he had lost the advantage of his position, and when Rupert was compelled to recross the plain he found his uncle's army in confusion. The Royal Standard had been captured, and Lord Lindsey was severely wounded in the thigh, and made a prisoner; and the king was himself in great danger of being taken, as he only had 100 horsemen about him. He would even then have continued fighting, so entirely was he a believer in the sacred invincibility of kings. Darkness helped the royal army, and, as Clarendon says, it was the darkness of an October evening which enabled the royal troops to hold their ground. Charles caused the cannon which were nearest to the enemy to be drawn off, and with his whole forces spent the night in the field, by such a fire as could be made of the little wood and bushes that grew thereabouts,' and in the morning both sides

claimed the victory; but the battle was not renewed. Lord Lindsey died in Essex's coach on his way to Warwick Castle, from the effects of his wound, and among others Sir Edward Verney, who carried the Royal Standard, was killed, and the following singular scene took place. Ensign Young took the standard and delivered it to Lord Essex, who handed it to his own secretary Chambers; but in the meantime one of the king's officers, Captain Smith, took the orange scarf from a fallen Parliamentarian, and passing himself off for one, he said that such a great trophy should not be in hands of a penman, and on securing it in the general confusion, he galloped back to the king, and was knighted on the spot.

Green, in his history, thus sums up the encounter: 'The two armies fell in with one another on the field of Edgehill, near Banbury. The encounter was a surprise, and the battle which followed was little more than a confused combat of horse. The moral advantage, however, rested with the king. Essex had learned that his troopers were no match for the cavaliers, and his withdrawal to Warwick left open the road to the capital.' The precise history of a battle, in which such fearful events are going on by the hour and minute, can never be written, as for example there might be two or three records of Waterloo all different, but all quite correct; and perhaps indeed there are, but nobody can ever reconcile them. All we know, and it is said that all the duke professed to be certain about, was the issue; but the localities of the civil wars, and the popular recollections of those who saw them, preserve a fairly correct narration.

Perhaps Edgehill is rather at a distance from Rugby, but the heights are clearly visible, and as the winding up of the war three years later was close to Rugby, the narration, with sketches, is given here. The war went on, and it greatly increased its area through the winter months, while its issues went steadily on for the king.

The queen arrived with arms from Holland, and thus greatly helped the royalists in their contests with the eastern counties. Lord Fairfax met with some reverses in the West Riding of Yorkshire, and Oxford was strongly fortified in his favour. Many circumstances that have come to light show how unfitted King Charles was for a ruler of the people.

Before the wars commenced the demands of both houses had, as it is said, 'risen' to require that they should have the power of appointing or dismissing the ministers of the crown, and that with them should rest the control of the military and civil affairs that concerned the welfare of the state; this, of course, is no more than the people at present are privileged to enjoy, but King Charles said that if he allowed such things he would be 'no more than the mere phantom of a king.' Into all his false promises and deceits during the troublous times it would be quite unnecessary to go, as also the battles that were won or lost; but, unhappily, the many shapely manor-houses that were wrecked, and the decorations of churches, and market crosses, and baronial residences like Warwick Castle, that were destroyed, was the work of Charles. But the finale of the wars brings us back closely to Rugby. Edgehill was fought on October 23, 1642, and Naseby, the final battle, occurred within three years, June 14, 1645, or just two centuries, less thirty years and four days before the battle of Waterloo. In its results, for all we can know, it was as important even as Bosworth, which happened within measurable distance.

The high table-land on which Naseby stands is really the central part of the watershed of England; some of the streams that rise here run east, such as the Nen and Welland, and others west. Locally, it is called the highest part of England, but this it is not by many degrees, if compared with the heights of Yorkshire or Cumberland. The successes had gradually been coming to Cromwell's armies, but as yet nothing could be certain, and even the battle of Naseby was an open event when it began. There is on the walls of Chester a tower called 'King Charles's Tower,' or sometimes 'Phœnix Tower,' and here Charles stood when he saw his forces utterly routed under Sir Marmaduke Langdale by General Poyntz, when they were on their way to reinforce the garrison of Chester. The town is not much altered, and resembles what it was when he saw his last battle.

Fortune had gone against Charles, and he had promised reforms and conciliations of all kinds in a conference that lasted for a long period in the picturesque old town of Uxbridge. The council-room where these meetings took place still stands, and is part of a country inn. 'But the hopes of concession which Charles had held out through the winter were suddenly withdrawn in the spring. He saw, as he thought, the Parliamentary army dissolved and ruined by the new modelling, at the instant when news came from Scotland of fresh successes on the part of Montrose, and of his overthrow of the Marquis of Argyll's troops in the victory of Inverlochy.' The 'new model, as it was called, had been adopted by Cromwell for a complete improvement in his army. It resembled the Ironsides in most respects, or the regiment of which Cromwell was the commander. He decided in the new model to get together an army of 20,000 men, who were all to be godly, sober, and honest, and his restrictions were such that Lords Manchester, Essex, and Waller resigned their commissions. Charles at once supposed that the day of Parliamentary power was over, and, of course, attached no importance to his promises of reform. Montrose said he would soon join him with a victorious army, and all offers of compromise or better government were at once abandoned. The tablet on the turret, which is just opposite the chapter-house of Chester Cathedral, says, 'King Charles stood on this tower, September 24, 1645, and saw his army defeated on Rowton moor.' Rowton moor is nearly three miles distant, and, though built over to some extent, it is in perfect prospect of the tower, which forms so prominent a feature on the Chester walls. But this occurred some three months after the battle of Naseby.

It was on the 7th of May that the King and Rupert left Oxford and went to raise the siege of Chester. This was his first visit, and he was successful; and when this was announced to the Parliamentary party, Fairfax, with his army,—which really was the new model,—was ordered to invest Oxford, and this he at once did. 'Charles advanced to Leicester and took it by storm; then, learning that Oxford was blockaded, he turned southward for the relief of that place, and established his headquarters at the Wheatsheaf Inn, Daventry,' and Fairfax marched from Oxford to meet him. When the news were received that the new 'model army was at hand,' a short council of war was held at the Wheatsheaf, and it was resolved, if possible, to avoid any encounter, but march into Yorkshire. This, however, was frustrated by Fairfax, who went from Oxford to meet him. Before the battle he had fallen upon a detachment of the Royal troops at Lutterworth and Naseby, and taken a number of prisoners.' The Naseby plateau extends from the village, northwards to beyond Sibbertoft where the hills slope down to the valley of the Welland. The plateau consists of a succession of low rolling hills with intervening valleys. 'A place of little hills and vales and some champein,' as one of the combatants described it. North of the village there is a slight depression, the ground rising again to Mill Hill, which is a mile from the church. Thence the ground slopes gently down in three successive waves, and finally rises again to Dust Hill. The distance between the tops of Dust Hill and Mill Hill is about a mile, and the intervening space called Broadmoor was the battlefield.

It would be soon after seven o'clock in the morning that Charles left Market Harboro' and marched to what finally was his doom. Rupert was in command, and Sir Jacob Astley, who, as Clarendon says, 'was an honest, brave, and plain man, and as fit for the office he exercised of major-general of foot as any man in Christendom yielded.' The cavalry on the left was commanded by Sir Marmaduke Langdale, whose complete overthrow at Chester Charles afterwards witnessed, and the right was commanded by Prince Rupert, and cut into two divisions or brigades, one under the leading of the Earl of Northampton and the other under Prince Maurice. There was also a reserve of horse under Colonel Howard, and still further in the rear was another reserve under Lord Lindsey, the son of the able

Market Harboro' from Brewery fields

general who received his death-wound at the battle of Edgehill. Indeed, if we look at the locality, we must admit that the Royal forces were well laid out. But then they had to contend with such leaders as Ireton, Fairfax, and Cromwell. Charles in armour and sword in hand, rode along the ranks of his army, and was received with great enthusiasm. 'Queen Mary' was the cry of the Royalists, and 'God is our strength,' that of the Parliamentarians. Ireton's division was completely routed by Rupert, and, as was their practice, the Royalist troops dismounted to plunder the waggons. Cromwell, on the other hand, attacked Sir Marmaduke Langdale, who led the right division, and quite routed him, and Fairfax, who had been with Cromwell, now turned to where the main battle was going on, and joined his forces with Skippon and Okey. Complete confusion soon came over the army of Charles, and the Royalists were utterly routed and fled. Rupert's men having completed their plundering, reformed, and were led back to the battle, and King Charles himself made a vigorous effort to recover the day, but it was too late, and the last hopes of the king were over, for after Naseby he was, as Sir Philip Warwick said, 'like a hunted partridge flitting from one castle to another.' Cromwell chased the defeated army as far as to Wigston Magna, but the king never drew in his reins until he had reached Ashby de la Zouche, somewhat over twenty-five miles from the scene of the battle. The result of the battle of Naseby is very extraordinary. It was estimated at the time that about 700 Royalists were killed in the battle, and 300 during Cromwell's pursuit. There were also 4500 prisoners taken, while the loss of the victorious army was only 200. The pedestrian may still see the *Sulby hedges*, by which Okey's dragoons were drawn up in line.

Naseby Church contains the remains of some Parliamentary officers. Some of their remains have been found, and bullets are frequently turned up in the cultivation of the soil, and the place where Royalists were carousing when Ireton fell in upon them is still perceived at Naseby Woolleys, a residence on the river Avon. The church itself had a long truncated spire, on which was fixed a hollow ball of copper. This was

Naseby Church.

brought from the capture of Boulogne which Henry VIII., when he had become an unwieldy monarch, managed to effect. Sir Giles Allingham, it is said, brought it and placed it on his house at Horseheath in Cambridgeshire, and when that was dismantled, Mr. Ashby secured it, and fastened it to the spire. The Ashbys belong to a very old Leicester family, and have had the Shrievalty of their county and occupied public offices during some centuries. A portion of this church was built in the fourteenth century, and there are yet some curious stilted pillars and some well-shaped caps.

Part of the Royalists found their way to Marston Trussel Church, which is called 'pudding poke Marston,' from the circumstance that the entrance to the church was finished in a *cul-de-sac*. In the flight of the troops after Naseby, a number of them sought refuge here, and they were simply cut to pieces by Cromwell's soldiers.

There is an old print of large dimensions that was published some short time after the battle, and under it is the following quaint description: 'The battle which gave the final turn to the King's affairs happened on the 14th June 1645; the first charge was given by Prince Rupert and his brothers, who bore down all before them, the left wing and the Northern horse engaging Cromwell and the Enemies' right wing, against odds of numbers and the advantage ground, were put to flight. The King, at the head of his reserve of Horse, was even ready to charge those which pursued his left wing, which might have recovered the misfortune when, on a Sudden, such a panic fear seized on them that they ran near a quarter of a mile without stopping, which happened upon an uncommon accident. For the Scotch Earl of Carnworth on a Sudden laid his hand on ye King's bridle, crying out with 2 or 3 oaths will you go to your Death in an Instant! and before his

Majesty understood what he would have, turned his Horse round, upon which a word run through the Troops, March to the Right, which, unfortunately, led them from charging the Enemy and assisting their own Men, and caused them all to turn their Horses and ride upon the spin as if every man was to shift for himself. After this Disorder the King, not being able to prevail with his troops to rally and charge the Enemy, he retreated as well as he could, and left Fairfax entire master of the field.'

There is a fine engraving of the battle of Naseby in Lord Clarendon's *History of the Grand Rebellion* in the print department of the British Museum.

COVENTRY

THE road from Rugby to Coventry is like the others in these parts, very delightful; perhaps the nearest is through Church Lawford and Binley, but possibly the one past Coombe Abbey is even more picturesque, while that to the south of them through Dunchurch and Ryton-on-Dunsmore is considered the old highroad.

The other places will be duly recorded afterwards. But of Ryton-on-Dunsmore we may say that it is a pleasant village about four miles from Coventry, and one of the twenty-four places given by Leofric to the monks of Coventry. In Edward I.'s reign, Thomas de Arden held the manor, and two mills, and certain lands belonged to the Abbey of Thorney of which the remains are so beautiful. A mill in those times was of feudal value, as tenants were bound to bring their produce to it. The church is dedicated to St. Leonard, and it contains some ancient monuments; it is partly built in the style of architecture that prevailed during the twelfth century. There is one great advantage in the Coventry roads, they all run nearly parallel to the railway, and about half-way between Rugby and Coventry is the picturesque village of Wolston, where there is a station, so that time may always be saved.

From Ryton-on-Dunsmore there is a fine prospect of Coventry with its three graceful spires. There are many versions of the old expression, 'Send him to Coventry,' but none of them are very explanatory or clear, yet the sentence is common all over England, quite as much so as 'Grinning like a Cheshire cat'; and though it may be slightly beyond the boundaries of the book, I may say what I think in spite of many theories on the subject, some of which even attach it to Cheshire cheeses sold in Bath with a cat embossed on them. The record of this day (January 29, 1891) reminds me of what I believe the real origin was: The exceeding cold has unearthed two real wild cats in Scotland, which are now in a national exhibition; and Delamere forest in Cheshire was perhaps the last place in England where these were found. It was almost the happy hunting-ground for the English squires and lords, and these wild cats especially were hunted down. They somewhat resembled in feature the Canadian laughing hyæna, and when parting with their nine lives, the hunters might well say with Warwick when speaking of Beaufort, 'See how the pangs of death do make him grin.'—*Henry VI.*

Until the year 1842, Coventry was a county in itself, the same as Chester. This distinction was conferred on it by Henry VI. in return for the loyalty of its citizens to his ambitious and restless wife, Queen Margaret of Anjou. The name of Coventry is spelled Conventry in old records, from the foundation, it is said, of a convent by Canute. St. Osburg was the Abbess in 1016, and then it was burned feloniously by Edric, who invaded Warwickshire, and did much damage to many of the towns. Unfortunately the amount of wood that figured in their construction then made them an easy prey to fire. On the site of the convent Leofric and his Countess Godiva erected a monastery which they endowed munificently. This was in the reign of Edward the Confessor. In 1355 Coventry was surrounded with walls which resembled in section those of Chester, but they were larger in circumference. Those of Chester are one and three-quarter miles, but those of Coventry were three miles in extent. For

three centuries the walls were kept in excellent repair, but evil days were before them. After Charles had erected his standard at Nottingham, he required the citizens to join his army, but when they refused he bombarded the city, though without effect.

On the restoration of Charles II., the inhabitants

made many enthusiastic demonstrations in his favour. The conduits, it is said, were made to flow with wine, and a basin and ewer with fifty pieces of gold were sent him as a memorial, and all the lands that were the king's lands were given up to him. But, perhaps because it was so near the scene of his father's final discomfiture, Charles was not to be appeased, and he ruthlessly sent the Earl of Northampton, with a large following of gentry and a detachment of troops, to break up the walls as a mark of his displeasure for the inhabitants not having taken the side of the royalists. This was done most ruthlessly. There was, except Chester, no other so completely walled city in England, and as the days ever since were days of peace, Coventry would have had another relic like the Chester walls. Three gates were spared, owing in all probability to the exhausted satiety of the destroyers. The city is charmingly situated on a gentle eminence, which is bounded on the north-east by the river Sherbourne and the Radford brook. The streets of Coventry are remarkable for their picturesque beauty, and the city is rich indeed that contains such noble buildings as St. Michael's Church and St. Mary's Hall, but quaint gables and artistic groups of old buildings meet the eye everywhere.

Coventry figures in *Richard II.* very remarkably; and we are almost surprised at this monarch's promptitude when his after career was so feeble, but then his amazing presence of mind when Wat Tyler was murdered by Walworth before them all, gave promise

of a future king that never was realised. 'My friends, be not concerned for the loss of your unworthy leader. I will be your leader.' This is the speech which history has put in his lips, but where we see any historical record in Shakespeare, we may be pretty sure that it rests on facts.

There is near Coventry a locality called Gosford Green, and here an old quarrel was to be decided between Henry Bolingbroke, the Duke of Hereford, who was the son of John of Gaunt, and Mowbray, the Duke of Norfolk; a throne was erected on which Richard sat when Norfolk entered, and he called out to the Lord Marshall:—

> 'Marshall, demand of yonder champion
> The cause of his arrival here in arms,' etc., etc.;

and he says of Bolingbroke when he enters with a herald:—

> 'Marshall, ask yonder knight in arms
> Both who he is, and why he cometh hither,
> Thus plated in habiliments of war,
> And formally, according to our law,
> Depose him in the justice of his cause.'

After all the preliminaries had been gone through and the charge was sounded the marshall calls out:—

> 'Stay, the king hath thrown his warder down;'

and then comes the memorable speech of Richard in which he banishes both of the combatants, Norfolk for life, and Bolingbroke, who afterwards deposed him, for ten years.

There is an account of this singular meeting in some old Warwickshire records that would throw much light upon the somewhat obscure opening of *Richard II.* in Shakespeare. The Duke of Hereford, who was afterwards Henry IV., is said to have had a private conversation with Mowbray, the Duke of Norfolk, which was of a treasonable character. Bolingbroke afterwards revealed this conversation, and all of his statements were quite denied by the Duke of Norfolk, who, in order to show his truthfulness, challenged him to a single combat, for in those days, and indeed even to later times, there was a belief that the battle was not to the strong, but to those who were in the right; and to illustrate how fanciful some of their views were, it might be added that there was a solemn engagement between the two combatants not to lend themselves to any chains of incantations, but to come fairly to the field without any undue magical influence. They then, it is stated, ignored any attempt to induce help from the lower regions, but required all good Christians to help them with their prayers :—

'Add proof unto my armour with thy prayers,
And with thy blessings steel my lance's point.'

About a mile after passing Ryton-on-Dunsmore we come to the river Avon, which here is in a pleasant valley, and soon after crossing the bridge that goes over it we arrive at a lane called Rowley Lane, from which we may have some fine views of the Coventry spires. A little more than a mile along this road will lead us to the very delightful village of Baginton, which s a little more than three miles to the south-east of Coventry. Turchil de Warwick possessed the manor in the days of William the Conqueror, and in Richard II.'s time Sir Walter Bagot was lord of the manor, and resided there; he was buried in the church, and a fine monumental brass was placed over him. The mansion was burned down, but it was rebuilt in Queen Anne's time by Bromley, the Speaker then of the House of Commons. In the grounds there are some remains of a castle where Henry Bolingbroke stayed when he left for Coventry, in September 1397, to meet Norfolk in mortal combat. He came on his white courser armed at all points, and well attended by his followers. Norfolk came from Caludon Castle on a horse trapped in crimson velvet, and embroidered with lions and mulberry leaves, alluding to his name Mowbray, or Mulberry.

Richard now entered Coventry. It was in the twentieth year of his reign, and he seems to have almost lost his self-control not long after. Hollinshead says that he came in great array accompanied with the lords and gentlemen of their lineages.

'The Duke of Hereford armed himself in his tent that was set up near to the lists. The Duke of Norfolk put on his armour behind the gate and the barrier of the town, in a beautiful house having a fair perclois of wood towards the gate, that none might see what was done within the house.

'The Duke of Aumerle that day being Constable of England, and the Duke of Surrey, Marshall, placed themselves betwixt them well armed and appointed.

'About the hour of prime the Duke of Hereford came to the barriers of the lists on a white courser. The Constable and Marshall came and demanded of him what he was. He answered: "I am Henry of Lancaster, Duke of Hereford, which am come thither to do my endeavour against Thomas Mowbray, Duke of Norfolk, as a traitor."

'Then incontinently he swore upon the holy evangelists that his quarrel was true and just. Then putting down his visor he descended spear in hand, and set him down upon a chair of green velvet at the end of the lists, and there reposed himself, abiding the coming of his adversary.

'Soon after him entered the field, and in great triumph, King Richard, accompanied with all the peers of his realm, and above ten thousand men in armour, lest some fray or tumult might rise among his nobles.

'The Duke of Norfolk hovered on horseback at the entrance of the lists; and when he had made his oath before the Constable that his quarrel was just, he entered the field manfully, calling aloud, "God aid him that hath the right!" and then he departed from his horse, and sat him down on his chair, which was crimson velvet. The Lord Marshall viewed the spears to see that they were of equal length. Then the herald proclaimed that the haverses and chairs should be removed, commanding them to mount on horseback and address themselves to the battle and combat.

'The Duke of Hereford was quickly horsed, and cast his spear into the rest, and when the trumpet sounded set forward courageously towards his opponent six or seven paces.' And now comes the singular scene which is always so comparatively puzzling in Shakespeare: the Duke of Norfolk was, as it seems, rather behindhand when the king suddenly cast down his warder, 'and the heralds cried Ho! ho! Then the king caused their spears to be taken from them, and commanded them to repair again to their chairs, where they remained two long hours, while the king and his council deliberately consulted what order was best to be had in so weighty a cause.' This is the account as given in Hollinshead's Chronicles, and it differs very little from Shakespeare's.

In Act I., Scene iii., Richard says :—

'Let them lay by their helmets and their spears,
And both return back to their chairs again.'

After a second consultation with his nobles, the king called the combatants, and said the quarrel must cease.

'And for our eyes do hate the dire aspect
Of civil wounds plough'd up with neighbours' swords.'

The two dukes were then banished, Hereford for ten years, and Norfolk for life. Gosford Green, where the event took place, lies just outside Coventry, on the road to Coombe Abbey.

There was a grand old cross at Coventry that stood at one time among the treasures of English architecture. It supplanted an old market-cross that rested on pillars and formed what is called a 'butter-market.' Happily, there are not a few of these crosses remaining, especially in the eastern and southern parts of England, and still they are used for market purposes; but the celebrated

Coventry cross was four stories in height. Its plan was hexagonal and it was fifty-seven feet high. Its niches were filled with statuary, and it was 'so highly illuminated with gold and colours that it was almost impossible to look upon it when the sun shone.' Every town in England then had its cross. In some, where the monastery had the privilege of the market dues, a monk or friar was told off on market days to preach against worldliness; but these crosses were always the places where public announcements were made—events that have nearly quite died out now, except in some very remote old towns. I have several times heard them. Bolingbroke, when Henry IV., said to Percy, the Earl of Worcester, as the latter called him to account for breaches of his promises of reform when they seated him on Richard's throne—

> 'These things, indeed, you have articulate,
> Proclaim'd at market-crosses, read in churches,
> To face the garment of rebellion
> With some fine colour.'

St. Mary's Hall, Coventry, is one of the most picturesque buildings that we have in any of our country towns. It was begun in 1394, and completed in 1414, on the site of an older hall. The buildings surround a courtyard and are approached by an archway from the street that has a finely carved entrance. It was erected for the united guilds of Trinity, St. Mary, John the Baptist, and St. Katherine, which became generally known as Trinity Guild, and is called by Dugdale, 'A fair and stately structure for their feasts and meetings;

situated opposite to St. Michael's Church.' On the dissolution of the Guild, the Corporation bought it, and have since used it as their hall. There are figures of the gentle Henry VI. and his warlike wife Margaret, and many other carved statues. Here, for a short time, Mary Queen of Scots was confined, and it is currently reported that her description of the spires enabled another generation to identify the place that she had been silently removed to. This was some time before she was taken to Fotheringhay Castle in Northamptonshire, which was the place where she ended her erring career.

St. Michael's Church is close by St. Mary's Hall, and is one of the finest parish churches in England. Many are the parish churches like Ludlow, or Yarmouth, or Nantwich, that would fill the status of a cathedral, and would indeed be purchased, if possible, at priceless sums by a new diocese such as Liverpool. But, of all the churches in England, it is somewhat doubtful if we have such a noble example of a parish church as St. Michael's, Coventry. It was begun, it seems, in 1372, a period with which the style quite corresponds, and finished twenty-two years later on by two brothers, William and Adam Botoner. They annually gave £100 for the completion of the grand building, and there is a brass plate that records their liberality :—

> 'William and Adam built the tower,
> Anne and Mary built the spire.
> William and Adam built the church,
> Anne and Mary built the quire.'

The church, fortunately, is open from ten o'clock to

four, and the view looking to the east is extremely grand. So light is the stonework, though it is abundantly strong, that it even looks from the chancel end almost like a huge bird-cage. The windows are finely decorated with stained glass and the view is well worth a pilgrimage. One of the windows is 'In memory of the great and good Albert Emanuel, Prince Consort

who entered immortality, December 1861.' The peal of ten bells is considered one of the finest in England. These were re-hung in 1794, but at present are on the floor of the church, it not having been thought good to re-hang them in the restored tower, upon a wooden framework rising from the ground so as not to disturb the delicate masonry of the tower. The spire is rather more than 300 feet in height, and is just of the same length as the church. The interior of the church derives much beauty from the tall, delicate piers which support the roof. The clerestory windows are double and very large, and indeed I cannot remember any church where the stone plays so small a part and the luminous remainder is so great. The living was valued in the king's books at £26, 15s. 4d. Now it is rated at £472, and it is still in the gift of the Crown.

Holy Trinity Church is a fine cruciform structure, which was valued in the king's books at £10, but now is worth £650, and it is in the patronage of the Lord Chancellor. The proportions are more massive than those of St. Michael's, but they are very fine. There is a monument to Dr. Philemon Holland on the south wall of the choir. He prided himself on having written a large book with one pen only, and thus he commemorates the event :—

> 'With one sole pen I wrote this book,
> Made of a grey goose quill.
> A pen it was when I it took,
> A pen I leave it still.'

This church is very richly endowed with estates, and there are numerous charities at its disposal.

There is a building of exceeding beauty and architectural merit—the Greyfriars' Hospital. This building has three gabled windows to the street, of very fine architectural proportions, and they project out artistically. The doorway, between two long ranges of windows, leads to the fine old court, which is shown, and which is a model of beauty and quaintness. It is quite free to enter, and well worth a long journey. The

woodwork is elaborately carved, and the heavy downspouts are quite made to compose with the rest of the architecture. The delicate oak carving round the frieze, and the charming light tracing in oak at the head of the windows should not be overlooked. This building was erected as a hospital, and is no part of a convent, though, indeed, it occupies the site of the Greyfriars' Monastery. The hospital was originally intended for the accommodation of aged men and women. It was built by William Ford in 1509 for five men and one woman to dwell in, and they were to have 5d. a week each for ever; and he ordered that lands and tenements should be purchased at the discretion of his executors for the payments. William Pisford, in compliance with this, by will, dated 1517, or eight years after the foundation, in his will extended the provisions of the rules for the admittance of inmates, and declared that these should be admitted into this guild, and said there should be six poor men and their wives, being nigh the age of threescore years, or above, and should have sevenpence halfpenny a week, and furthermore, if the wife of any should die before her husband, he should have the sevenpence halfpenny a week; but if the men left widows, these were to receive but threepence halfpenny per week, and two that were similarly left should live together.

Coventry was the seat of Parliament on various occasions. The Lancastrian kings summoned Parliament here, and well the citizens remembered their good offices when their days were troubled. But Parliaments were held here, one by Henry IV. and his descendants, and they had singular names. One Parliament excluded all lawyers from sitting among them, and it was called in consequence the 'Parliamentum Indoctorum.' Of course the 'Indoctorum' did not so much refer to the want of learning in the members as to the absence of legal knowledge. Another Parliament was called the 'Parliamentum Diabolicum,' which name was given in consequence of the severe measures that were passed by it against the Duke of York and his adherents. The king, Henry VI., had become very unwell, and the Duke of York, as a descendant of Edmund Langley, quietly put in his claim to the future monarchy, and his claim was rather popular. The king was so unwell as to be almost incapable for a year, and York was appointed the protector of the realm. On the king's recovery, Somerset, who had been committed to the Tower, was restored to power, and York took up arms. Somerset fell, and a renewal of the king's malady restored York to power; but the recovery of the king caused his overthrow, and he fled to Ireland, when the queen summoned a parliament to Coventry, and all sorts of harsh attainders were passed against the Yorkists.

WARWICK

HAPPILY the attention of England is being turned to its own native architecture, and the picturesque old towns that still bear traces of former days. At the beginning of the Tudor period, the architecture, which is called perpendicular, was in its best form, though, as it now seems, there are excellent examples of it which date before the fourteenth century was advanced very far, as the Dean of Gloucester informs us from examples and records that he has in Gloucester Cathedral. The perpendicular style is entirely English, and not seen on the Continent; for when it appeared the Flamboyant took its place there. It was in Elizabeth's time that the 'grand tour' became so necessary as an accomplishment to young men of wealth, and the singular part of the record is that, unlike the men of other countries, they did not even attempt, as they might have done, to master the languages of the Continent, or even to read the Latin language with its accents and pronunciation of vowels, as they should, and as others did, and even yet do. There is a passage in the *Merchant of Venice* that throws much light upon the strange mixture of the English and foreign habits and styles that were being merged into our own ways of life. Nerissa says, 'What say you to Falconbridge, the young baron of England?' and Portia replies, 'You know I say nothing to him, for he understands not me, nor I him; he hath neither Latin, French, nor Italian, and you will come into the court and swear that I have a poor pennyworth in the English. He is a proper man's picture; but, alas, who can converse with a dumb-show? How oddly he is suited! I think he bought his doublet in Italy, his round hose in France, his bonnet in Germany, and his behaviour everywhere.' There is hardly anything that throws a more clear light than this upon the change that was coming over England. Every county then contained many examples of picturesque baronial mansions, some of which happily remain, and there were in Elizabeth's reign great numbers of monasteries that had been transformed into residences, and were almost priceless examples of English architecture. But the country was then very wealthy, and the returning travellers brought with them designs to destroy their ancestral homes. Hence the Elizabethan style began, which was a blending of Gothic and Italian; and, indeed, if we take such a building as Wollaton, near Nottingham, we shall see the work of two architects apparently contemporaneous, one of whom is desirous to adhere to Gothic forms, even modified, while the other desires the Italian to prevail. But the spirit of Italianising advanced with time, and the Hanoverian architecture which prevailed in the days of the the first Georges wrecked countless old country mansions that now would be the goal of a pilgrimage. In Cheshire there are many such destructions, but we have such relics as Bramhall and Moreton still entire, and, indeed, many others. There is some little difference of opinion as to which is the most antique-looking town or city in England, but I think the selection rests with four—Warwick, Coventry, Shrewsbury, and either Salisbury or Wells. Chester, where this is written, is sadly over-rated as an example of antiquity; the walls are Roman, but much altered even to the present time,

Leicester's Hospital.

and the rows, curious as they are, have been nearly all rebuilt. Leicester's hospital in Warwick has few parallels in quaint architecture, and the tunnel walk under the chapel is of intense picturesque beauty.

This hospital was founded by the Lord Leicester, whose name is so sadly connected with his Countess, Amy Robsart, and the foundation-stone was laid in the twenty-eighth year of Elizabeth's reign. It was endowed for twelve indigent men, and was endowed well with property, including buildings belonging to the Guild. The building encloses a quadrangle, and on either side there is a covered passage of wood that leads to the apartments of the brethren. These must have been for at least five years resident in Warwick, Kenilworth, Stratford-on-Avon, or else in the manors of Arlingham or Wotton-under-Edge in Gloucestershire. All of the recipients are clothed in blue cloth gowns, and they have the founder's arms in silver—the bear and ragged staff. As it is in other local hospitals and alms-houses, the residents must declare themselves to be in want, and under no circumstances to possess more than five pounds a year. Those were to have the preference who had been wounded or disabled in the service of their country. There was, at one time, in the kitchen garden, a Nilometer, or a record tablet that showed the rise of the Nile, a circumstance that was always a puzzle to the ancients, who saw a river of 700 miles long without a feeder worth notice, and not subject to showers or rains, but passing through the dryest of parched lands, and yet overflowing its banks annually for miles, and fertilising the country. They knew nothing then of the great lakes from which the Nile receives its supplies, and which are overwhelmed with water in the rainy season.

> 'Wise ancients knew when Crater rose to sight,
> Nile's festive deluge had sustain'd its height.'

This relic was presented to the hospital by the Earl of

Warwick, who supplanted it in his garden at Warwick Castle by the celebrated Warwick vase. The residence of the master occupies the great part of the court, and it bears also the badge of the Leicesters, and the date of the foundation. In St. Mary's Church there are seats allotted to the brethren, which they use on stated occasions. It is a well-known edifice, and well worthy of a visit. It is also called the High Church, and has had

many phases of existence. It is mentioned in Domesday Book; but it was repaired, if not rebuilt, in Stephen's time, and in 1394 the church was rebuilt by Thomas Beauchamp, the founder of the magnificent Beauchamp Chapel which still remains, and is one of the treasures of England. The building was nearly destroyed by fire in 1694, but it was rebuilt and opened up in 1704, with such Gothic as the period afforded. Fortunately, however, the grand Beauchamp Chapel, and the chapter-house and vestry, escaped. When the brethren do not attend at the High Church they go to their own chapel, which figures with such great beauty at the entrance to Warwick. Services, when not held at the High Church, are held here, and the brethren attend at morning and evening. This chapel was modernised by Sir Gilbert Scott, and stained glass put in the east window. James I. visited Warwick, and was received with great ostentation at the hospital. The architecture of the hospital is excellent, the gables are shapely and beautifully grouped. The upper part of the court-yard front, which is shown, is admirable, but the lower part has rather too much variety in arrangement. It is a great mistake to suppose that irregularity is a desirable feature in English architecture, and this is beginning now to be understood; the picturesque charms of the best examples result from this: the plan of the building is made to suit the requirements, and the exterior is made as congruous and harmonious as the circumstances will permit. Where, as in such a front as Versailles, the other course prevails, the long rows of enormous windows have often to rule the plan, and one of them is perhaps cut in two internally by a partition wall, and lights a footman's pantry and a stairway. Some of the best and most artistic of the oak and plaster work, which is also called magpie, and post, and petrel work is to be seen in Cheshire, when the vast oak-trees of Delamere were in vigorous growth. The Earl of Leicester, who founded and endowed the hospital, is almost immortalised by

Scott in *Kenilworth*, and his treatment of Amy Robsart, and his ambitious designs to let Queen Elizabeth take her place, are too well known to need repetition here.

The church at Cumnor, near Oxford, is well worthy of a visit, and is delightfully situated, and here it was that Amy Robsart lived ; the south transept that butts into the park is the same as when she saw it, and indeed it was then two centuries old. It does not appear in Sir Walter Scott's novel, but at the request of her father the body was disinterred from St. Mary's Church, and an inquest was held. Of course it would not have been possible to have brought in any word that would have compromised the Earl of Leicester, whose chaplain, Dr. Babington, had preached her funeral sermon, and it was supposed to be all hushed up ; but the jury, guided by the coroner, had the courage to say that she was 'accidentally slain'; and that conveys enough to us now. Anthony Foster, who was undoubtedly the culprit, is buried in Cumnor Church ; and on the north side of the chancel there is a monument of grey marble, and on it there is a man in armour and his wife, dressed in the habit of the times, and under them is the Latin inscription :—

> 'Antonius Foster, generis generosa propago,
> Cumnerae dominus, Bercheriensis erat.
> Armiger, armigero prognatus patre Ricardo,
> Qui quondam Iphlethæ Salopiensis erat.
> Quatuor ex isto fluxerunt stemmate nati,
> Ex isto Antonius stemmate quartus erat.
> Mente sagax, animo precellens, corpore promptus ;
> Eloquii dulcis, ore disertus erat.

> In factis probitas ; fuit in sermone venustas,
>   In vultu gravitas, relligione fides,
> In patriam pietas, in egenos grata voluntas,
>   Accedunt reliquis annumeranda bonis.
> Si quod cuncta rapit, rapuit non omnia Lethum,
> Si quod mors rapuit, vivida fama dedit.'

How far this is just, I think any reader of *Kenilworth* can say. But in an after-note to *Kenilworth*, it is said that, 'Notwithstanding the charity, benevolence, and religious faith imputed by the monument to its tenant, tradition, as well as secret history, name him as the active agent in the death of the Countess.'

Some years ago, when I was at Oxford, it was my lot to fall in at a farmhouse with a very old resident, who had a curious history to tell. He had been at one time the butler to Pembroke College, and when I saw him he was in his ninety-eighth year, and within a few days of the end even of that, but he was in sound health. He remembered a considerable part of Cumnor Hall standing, and quite well the private chapel where the grain, in after years, was stowed. He also remarked that the trees in the park were not oaks, as Scott and Mickle had stated in their records, but elms, as indeed we can see them now. But, as I once wrote before, 'This aged chronicler mentioned a curious circumstance that illustrates the last verse of Mickle's beautiful ballad of Cumnor Hall.' It was indeed a ballad that suggested *Kenilworth* to Scott:—

> 'And in that Manor now no more
>   Is merry feast or sprightly ball,
> For ever since that dreary hour
>   Have spirits haunted Cumnor Hall.'

He said that in his young days, which would be sometime in the latter part of the eighteenth century, much of Cumnor Hall was left, and also there were among other things some artificial ponds for fish such as were common in old times in great houses when there was no fish market or trains to bring sea-fish into the country parts, and so the country houses had to provide for themselves. He remembers that he and his village compatriots used to go and fish in these ponds, and it was a case for immediate running away when one of the party used to call out, 'Madame Dudley is coming.'

Warwick is only a short distance by rail, but there is a very pleasant road to it by Dunchurch, Prince Thorpe, Wapenbury, and Cubington. Here there is a fine church with two stained-glass windows and an excellent chancel. In the reign of Henry III. this manor was divided between the Prior of Coventry and Henry de St. Maure. He, it would seem, committed a murder, and his lands were conveyed to the Crown, and afterwards they were bestowed on the Knights Templars. Near here is 'Lovers' Grove,' as it is called, which has a number of delightful views of the surrounding country.

If in place of going to Warwick it should be decided to visit the grand old castle of Kenilworth, a walk of exceeding beauty would take us through the grounds of Stoneleigh Abbey to the historic abode of Kenilworth. The park round Stoneleigh is very extensive and well stocked with deer and venerable oak trees. There is, as there should be and perhaps now is through most great parks, a road where the pedestrian may go ; and this is not a great way from Rugby, and stations are near. Ashow is a small rural village with the interesting church of St. Mary, and it is situated in a beautifully secluded spot on the banks of the Avon, and so far back as the reign of Henry II. it was conveyed to the canons of Kenilworth, and here Henry II. founded an abbey for Cistercian monks. This order always chose the most beautiful of spots for their house, and their architecture is exceedingly graceful and fine, besides being of the highest class of masonry.

Their monastery has, however, disappeared, though there are some remains of it left among the domestic offices that afford good examples of Norman work, but in its place we have the magnificent residence called Stoneleigh Abbey, of which a sketch is given, and it is certainly one of the finest country seats in England. There are two rather severe-looking classic lodges on the Warwick road, and between them is the principal entrance to the so-called 'Abbey,' a name that does not certainly agree with its Roman front. This building was erected in the early part of last century, but it has undergone many changes since. There are rooms in it that are open to the public, and perhaps the most interesting features in these are the pictures. In the picture gallery there is a portrait of the second Lord Rockingham and his wife, who was a daughter of the notable Earl of Strafford who was beheaded in the time of Charles I. The billiard-room has many ancestral portraits of the Leigh family and the Dukes of Buckingham. There are also works of Cuyp, Teniers, Vandyck, Albert Durer, and other great artists, and there is a picture of the Virgin and Child by Perugino. The private apartments are of equal magnificence with those to which the public are admitted, and the gardens are laid out in admirable style.

The history of the Leigh family is very interesting. They belong to the great Cheshire families of Leigh who have so many seats in that county. Sir Thomas Leigh was Lord Mayor of London in 1558, and was knighted during his mayoralty. He died on the 17th November 1571, and was buried in the Mercer's Chapel in London, with the following inscription on his tomb:—

> 'Sir Thomas Leigh bi civil life
>   All offices did beare,
> Which in this city, worshipfull,
>   Or honorable were.
> Whom as God blessed with great wealth,
>   So losses did he feele,
> Yet never changed his constant minde
>   Though fortune turned her wheele.
> Learning he loved, and helpte the poore,
>   To them that knew him deere,
> For whom his lady and loving wife
>   This tomb hath builded here.'

The family were raised to the peerage in 1643 by Charles I., as the patent dated at Oxford shows, and he married one of the daughters and co-heirs of Sir Thomas Egerton, a niece of the great chancellor. Edward, the fifth Lord Leigh, died unmarried in 1786, at the age of forty-four, and the barony became extinct. But there is another link between these two families. Sir William Leigh of Newnham Regis, one of the Leighs of Stoneleigh, married a daughter of Lord Ellesmere, a name that is yet illustrious even among the chancellors of England. About seven miles from Chester there is a secluded country church well shaded with trees and far from a railway station; here the chancellor lies buried. There is a monument to him, and the sexton showed me the register of his burial in the church books.

The foundation of Stoneleigh as an abbey may be told in Dugdale's words: 'The order of Cistercian monks being propagated in England towards the latter part of Henry I.'s reign found in a short time many pious benefactors in several parts of the kingdom, who bountifully bestowed on them very valuable possessions in such places as were most proper for them to seat themselves with least disturbance in their strict and holy rule of serving God, amongst which were the empress and King Stephen, who, though otherwise opposite to each other, yet in this good work concurred, granting a certain desert called Redmore, lying in the forest of Canok in Staffordshire, a mile southwards from Beaudesart, unto Clement and Herveie, two devout hermits, with others of their society, as also a certain land called Mellescho for tillage and pasturage of cattle; which concessions Roger de Clinton, then Bishop of Chester, not only confirmed, but gave them liberty to betake themselves to what regular life soever they thought God's direction should make choice of, and to receive and instruct any such women, who, having devoted their lives to God's service, should do the like.

'But after they found what molestation they had by the foresters, who, riding frequently that way, much disturbed their devotions, they humbly sought the empress that she would vouchsafe to change their seat.

'Whereupon, having a great affection for the Cistercian Order, she told them if they would undergo that Rule she would grant their request. To which proposal of hers, they after some deliberation assenting, the same place of Radmore was made an Abbey, one William, the principal of those religious persons, being elected the first Abbot there, unto whom Henry, Duke of Normandy, son to the said empress, by his charter granted and confirmed not only the same Radmore with the appurtenances, viz., Melescho and Wirley for tillage and pasture, and also Hedensford for pasturage and pannage, with liberty to build a church, and such houses as might be fit for their habitation, but gave them the town of Canok with the appurtenances, and the mill at Wirley with all things belonging thereto.

'Which good work so begun wanted but the bounty of divers other pious men to carry it on: Osbern de Aidern giving them his lordship of Merston ; William Croe all the right he had in Wirley, to the intent that they should receive him into their fraternity and vouchsafe his body burial there ; Geoffrey de Clinton, Bishop of Chester, beforementioned, two hides more in the said town of Radway.

'Shortly after this said new Abbot and his monks, not yet well instructed in the Cistercian discipline, requested Hamon, the second abbot of Bordesley in Worcestershire, to send two of his convent to inform them therein. Which being accordingly done there grew great friendship between these two monasteries, the monks of Bordesley giving courteous entertainment to those of Radmore whensoever they had occasion to visit their grange at Radway. Howbeit at Radmore they continued no more than twelve years, for, finding the foresters not only troublesome, but by their frequent visits somewhat burdensome also, they became petitioners to King Henry II., on the 14th kal. of January, in the very first year of his reign, making use of his mother the empress, their patroness, to mediate, that he would be pleased to translate to them his manor of Stoneley in Warwickshire, and accept what they had at Radmore in exchange for that place. Whereunto, the king graciously yielding, they came from Radmore and first seated themselves where the Grange of Cryfield now stands, the inhabitants thereof then removing to Hurst. But finding inconvenience there in regard that it was so near the public roadway, they made choice of another place a little below the confluence of the Sow and Avon, almost environed with the river, having that thick wood called Echells on the north. And then began the foundation of their church, whereof the first stone was laid id. Apr. Anno 1154, scil. 1 Henry II. The churchyard was consecrated by Walter Durdant, Bishop of Coventry, with the assent of the prior and canons of Kenilworth, to whom the parish church of Stoneley appertained, upon condition that the said monks should in no way diminish the rights due to the said church of Stoneley, but make just payment of all tithes to the same for such grounds as they should till within the parish, all of which the said King Henry by his charter confirmed.'

This is a very excellent account of the formation of a Cistercian Abbey, one that is very characteristic of the order, and we might almost tell a Cistercian Abbey from its quiet and beautiful situation.

Guy's Cliff is half-an-hour's walk from Warwick on the Kenilworth road, and it is among the most beautiful of all the pleasant spots of England. The renowned Guy, Earl of Warwick, lived here, and there is a cave near the banks of the Avon where it is said he was buried. Here he is said to have lived in retirement and devotion, and to have adopted the garb of a hermit, but every day he visited the castle where his countess dwelt. 'Near the cave is a range of cells having the appearance of a nunnery, and some cloisters hewn in the rock and rudely arched, called Phillis cloisters, after the countess, who survived him only a few days, and was buried near him.' Guy's Well contains a fine spring of the clearest water known. Camden speaks of it as 'the very seat of pleasantness,' and Dugdale says, 'A place this of so great delight, in respect of the river gliding below the rock, the dry and wholesome situation, and the fair grove of lofty elms overshadowing it, that to one who desireth a retired life, either for his devotions or his study, the like is hardly to be found.' The mansion itself is not quite an example of an old residence, but it was erected during the last century by Mr. Samuel Greathead, who purchased the property, and is not a bad example of the architecture that then prevailed.

Henry V., it is said, made a pilgrimage here, and he was so delighted with the quiet sequestered spot that he founded a chantry for three priests. He did not live to complete his intentions, but Richard Beauchamp, the Earl of Warwick, appointed two priests to celebrate mass for himself and his countess, and after their death this was to be continued for them and the souls of the departed.

The estate afterwards became the property of Lord Charles Percy through marriage, and remains in that family. There are pictures of considerable value in the house, but the most remarkable is probably the portrait of Mrs. Siddons, who, as Miss Kemble, lived in the capacity of lady's-maid to Mrs. Greathead before her marriage with Mr. Siddons. The avenue of elms through which the mansion appears is very fine, but the old mill which is here shown is even more picturesque. This mill has a history that dates back to the Conquest. Nearly opposite Guy's Cliff in a hollow part of the rock is the place where the worthless Piers Gaveston met his end, and a monument has been put up by Bertie Greathead with a very suitable inscription.

STONELEIGH ABBEY

At the same time when this monastery was so founded there were in the manor of Stoneleigh sixty-eight villeins, four bordarii (that is, freeholders), and two priests, all which held thirty-two carucates of land (as expressed in Domesday Book). 'As also four bondsmen or servants, whereof each held one mess, and one quartrone of land, by the services of making the gallows and hanging the thieves, every one of which bondsmen was to wear a red clout betwixt his shoulders on his upper garment; to plow twice a year; to reap as often—that is to say, at the two bederipes; to give aid to the lord at the feast of St. Michael; to make the lord's malt, and to do other servile work.'

There are a few records in Dugdale of the abbots. One, who is described as of singular wisdom, Will de Gyldforde, the ninth abbot, was sent with legatine authority to Wales, 'which occasioned many superior abbots to malign him, so that because he countenanced a shepherd belonging to the monastery to fight a duel, and hang a thief that had privately stolen some cattle of theirs, much advantage was taken against him such as that, being persecuted for it, he was deprived in anno 1235, 19th Henry III. 'Within ten years of this the monastery suffered from fire, and the king allowed them fifty oaks out of his woods at Kenilworth, which the sheriff of this county had command to deliver.' The building must have been extremely grand, for this is the time when English architecture was in its glory. Rickman, who was the first to discriminate the styles of architecture methodically, and to give the names of Early English, Decorated, and Perpendicular, places this date at the Early English period, or that which he considers ranged from Richard I., 1189, to Edward I., 1307. Excellent indeed Rickman's analysis is, and indeed the best, though perhaps later records might show, as he himself would have at once admitted, that there is not always a rigid barrier between the styles.

In this time we have the north transept of York Minster, the north aisle of Croyland, and the ruins of the grand abbey of St. Mary's, in York—ruins that still are sharp and clear in their carvings, and, indeed, any one who will compare the remains of this date with the later architecture that we find in abbey enlargements of the Tudor period, will be surprised at the wide difference in the workmanship, though perhaps in the parish churches it is more apparent. But I have seen in the same town the remains of thirteenth century architecture and Tudor, the latter falling to decay while the former, the work of the monks of that period, was perfect, and the lines of the columns almost like brass mouldings for correctness.

This may be said of St. Mary's ruins at York, the ruins of one of the only two mitred abbeys north of the Trent, and this abbey was approaching completion at about the same time as the new additions were being made to Stoneleigh. St. Alban's Abbey, at any rate as far as the choir is concerned, was built at this time, and many other ecclesiastical structures that adorn England. Within a few miles round Rugby we could find sufficient remains of English architecture to write and fully illustrate a work upon the subject.

It will be noticed that in the hilly countries the churches generally have a tower, and we may notice this especially round Rugby where the land is hilly ; but as

Stoneleigh Abbey.

we approach the flat country in Northamptonshire, spires prevail. Round Oakham and Stamford spires are entirely the rule, and some of the finest examples of these that England can show are here.

Salisbury spire is a landmark of the almost roadless plain, and has for centuries been the guide of farmers and shepherds when away from home ; and admirably it suits the solitary landscape. If we want an example to the contrary we might look at the Acropolis. Salisbury spire, and all the Northampton ones, would appear insignificant there among the rough cliffs. It requires a very different style to suit the scene and make a proper contrast. In Athens the long lines of the Parthenon and the surroundings form the most impressive picture, and a fine resting-place for the eye to dwell on. And perhaps a slight digression on the subject of Greek architecture might not be quite out of place, as there are many Greek buildings in this part of England. This class of architecture is quite unsuited to our country. It does not blend with the landscape and has an exotic appearance always. We often see in towns a Greek pediment supported by Doric or Ionic columns, and fronting a chapel or some other building. It may be, as it probably generally is, that this is an exact copy of some Greek building, such as the Agora, or the Ionic temple on the Ilissus, or perhaps the temple of Theseus, on a small scale, but it is sadly out of place, and quite out of keeping with the climate and the country, and even the materials of which such buildings are constructed.

If we look at the streets of Coventry or Warwick with all their picturesque surroundings, we shall feel pleasure and delight, instead of the chill which a Grecian front gives us on an English street.

Perhaps the most striking example of this is the well-known St. George's Hall in Liverpool. As an example of Greek architecture it is very high indeed. The gables and excellent Corinthian columns, and all its fine perspectives, are worthy of all praise; but does it suit its locality? The architecture itself would have deserved a place, and that a high one, on the Acropolis, but it is already dimmed with town atmosphere, and the slight appearance of Greek character, when the stone (though not white marble) was fresh, has vanished.

> 'Decay's effacing fingers
> Have swept the lines where beauty lingers . . . .
> Such is the aspect of this shore ;
> 'T is Greece, but living Greece no more.'

We should have to revert, in imagination, to the times when Athens was in its grandeur, to at all understand Greek architecture. As Stuart, who is the best authority we have on the styles and their origins, points out, the Greeks determined the site of their cities rather from the position of some isolated rock than by the wants of domestic or commercial accommodation. ' Even when, as in Athens, the neighbourhood of a commodious haven may have formed one strong inducement to the choice of a particular locality, the settlers rejected the obvious expediency of occupying the shore for the greater security of some rugged elevation.' But the temples were of fine white marble, and the sunshine of Greece lit them up always with a brilliant front such as we could never attempt to equal in England.

That the temples were painted in gay colours has often been said, and there are doubtless the remains of bright paint on the columns and cornices, but these have certainly been added since. Would Praxiteles not have known, for example, the value of the beautiful shadows of fine Pentelican marble? The Turks in their possession of Athens, doubtless had something to do with the colouring, and they broke to pieces very many priceless relics. The magnificent entrance to the Erechtheum was quite out of sight when Stuart visited Athens, for the portico had been walled up and made to serve the purposes of a powder magazine. One good end seems to have been served, however, for it is now in excellent preservation. The Elgin Marbles are quite as much out of place in the British Museum as a picture of Millais would be in a cellar. They were cut for the bright suns of Greece. The figures are raised by almost right angular elevations from the surface of the frieze, so as to throw out their forms in shadows at any distance to those with clear sight. And as for the absolute technical accuracy of the Greek details, the volute of an Ionic column is given in decimals in *Chambers*, and so intense is the precision that, as the writer knows, it takes several days to work out an Ionic capital if such records are followed, though now they perhaps never are.

Widely all this differs from the architecture of our own country. Here the ancient buildings even gain in merit by the time-stains, and the dwellers in many a country village have been saddened by the scraping off of all traces of antiquity in their parish church, and the destruction of the black oak pews where their grandfathers worshipped.

The very atmosphere which gave Greece, and to some extent Rome, its merit and beauty, is reversed in England, for here the time-stains and lichens give our old buildings even more than half their beauty. A very slight introduction to the forms of our own architecture would suffice to interest all travellers, and greatly increase their interest in any English ramble. There are the round Norman arches with their many devices, the Early English or Lancet, as it is sometimes called, and the 'Decorated,' which is perhaps the least applicable term of Rickman's, though his knowledge has made it a dictionary word.

At the dissolution the revenues of Stoneleigh Abbey were valued at £178, 2s. 5d., which of course is a fraction of what such a sum would represent now. Often we see in guide-books the value of the revenues of an abbey at the dissolution, and are surprised that the noble buildings could even have lasted for a year with such a slight income, but there are many circumstances to be considered.

There is no doubt that the Crown commissioners' valuation in the Tudor days went strongly in favour of the abbeys, and then there is one heavy item omitted, and that is the large income that was received from guests or travellers who put up in the hospitium, or guests' hall. Of course the value of a pound was very much greater in those days than it is now. Some say that it was twenty times as much, and some estimate it at half that amount, but no just estimate can be made of the difference. It varied much in different parts of the kingdom, as indeed some similar examples may be found in the present day, and that, too, where steam has done so much to assimilate prices; for even now there are country districts in England where money will go half as far again as it would do in some of our great towns. But in old times the difference was infinitely greater, and that leads to confirm what was said, that there is no possibility of gauging the difference between the old and the present values of money by any equational system.

But there is another circumstance that is omitted in the valuations of the religious houses: all around the monasteries there were great lands and farms attached, and these were tilled by the monks, the fruit and vegetables and poultry and cattle not only supplied all the wants of the abbey or priory, but, in many cases, there was a considerable surplus for the market. The monks were trained also in trades and crafts, which, as we may see even now, were carried to great perfection. Those who were so employed were not obliged to attend devotions, but when the convent bell rang they ceased from their work for a little time and assumed a devotional attitude till the bell ceased.

These circumstances would greatly explain the apparently small rent-rolls of abbeys that possessed buildings of palatial splendour, and the estates of which in the Tudor times enriched the wealthier of all the English nobles, and the revenues which they brought show clearly enough how lenient the estimates of Henry's commissioners were. The ways of the abbots and priors were not so strict in the Tudor times as they were in the days of the Edwards; and in looking over some records of the commissioners that we have in Chester, I wish I could say that the lives of the dignitaries, at the time of the dissolution, were all quite free from blame.

In the earlier days of Erasmus, the 'New learning was received well by princes and bishops, and even by some popes who hoped to improve the reforms that were going on. But the monastic orders were against the new training, with some few exceptions.' Even Sir Thomas More, whose name will always stand among the foremost of Englishmen, and who was a consistent Catholic, had much to say about the condition of monasteries: 'The friar, now that his fervour for devotion and his intellectual energy had passed away, had sunk into the mere beggar. The monks had become mere landowners. Most of the houses were anxious only to enlarge their revenues, and to diminish the number of those who shared them. In the general carelessness which prevailed as to the religious objects of their trust, in the wasteful management of their estates, in the indolence and self-indulgence which for the most part characterised them, the monastic houses simply exhibited the faults of all corporate bodies which have outlived the work they were created to perform. But they were no more unpopular than such corporate bodies generally are.' In many parts of England, monasteries were supplied with schools to educate the families of country gentlemen.

Now, it may be just appropriate to mention here, as we are in the land of abbeys, that two royal commissioners, Legh and Leyton, had been despatched to visit the religious houses generally. The report formed what is called the 'black book,' which was laid before the house. The greater part of the larger abbeys were well conducted, as well as some few of the smaller ones, making in all, it is said, about one-third of the number; but it was alleged, and it is to be feared, that there was but too much truth in some of the reports of the royal commissioners.

Near the entrance of Stoneleigh is the village of Ashow, a very pleasant spot. The church is dedicated to St. Mary, and it has a square tower like others in the district. This formerly was a chapel belonging to Wooton, but Henry II. conferred it upon the canons of Kenilworth. The situation is a quiet secluded one on the banks of the Avon, and its picturesque beauty is well worthy of a visit. On the other side of Stoneleigh, and situated some little distance away, is the village of Stoneleigh.

It stands at the confluence of the Sow and the Avon, and just below an old water-mill. The church also is dedicated to St. Mary, and its ivy-mantled tower is very interesting. It has a nave and chancel and side aisles, and its tower, supported by heavy buttresses, is very curious. It is surmounted by another of smaller dimensions crowned with pinnacles at the angles; between the nave and chancel is a large Norman arch, richly ornamented, and supported by columns of which the shafts and capitals are greatly embellished. Round the east end is a series of small Norman arches, or perhaps transitional would be the better term. On the north side of the chancel is the mausoleum of the Leigh

Stoneleigh Abbey.

family, the ceiling of which is beautifully worked in groined and ribbed arches. The south aisle is separated from the nave by three pointed arches, supported on octagonal pillars. In the chancel is a splendid monument to the memory of Lady Alice, Duchess Dudley, also a recumbent figure found in an upright position in a wall while digging the foundation of the mausoleum. It is supposed to be in memory of Geoffrey de Muschamp, Bishop of Coventry and Lichfield in the reign of John. The living is now a vicarage, valued at £303 per annum. It is in the gift of Lord Leigh, and the rectory is a pleasant house near the church. We are, when at Stoneleigh, not more than a mile and a half from Baginton, another village of picturesque beauty. The road follows the course of the river Sow, and has many charming scenes. At one place there is an oak tree that formerly belonged to the old forest of Arden, and is said to be the only relic of that ancient cover.

The church of Baginton is dedicated to John the Baptist, and belongs to the thirteenth century. It is about three and a half miles from Coventry, and at the Conquest it belonged to Turchil de Warwick. In the sixth year of Richard II., Sir William Bagot was Lord of the Manor, and lived at the castle of which some very slight traces remain. It was from here that the Duke of Hereford proceeded to Gosford Green, near Coventry, for his intended combat with the Duke of Norfolk. In the reign of James I., William Bromley purchased the manor, and his grandson was appointed Speaker of the House in the ninth year of Queen

Anne's reign. While he was Speaker of the House, the old family mansion was destroyed by fire, and the present mansion was erected on its site. It stands on an eminence on the Coventry road, and commands a fine view of the three spires, about which so much has been written. The residence is approached by a noble avenue of chestnut and other trees, and near it is a fine cedar that is said to have been planted by Queen Anne when on a visit to Speaker Bromley. Sir William Bromley, Knight Commander of the Bath, by deed dated 1675, granted some valuable tithes and rent-charges to the incumbent and poor of Baginton.

A pleasant walk from Baginton along Rowley Lane will bring us in a little over a mile to the Coventry road, that which comes directly through Dunchurch from Rugby. If we turn to the left, we cross the river Sow, and pass by Whitley Abbey, which lies near Coventry. This abbey belonged to Viscount Hood, who was a son of the brave admiral that gained so decisive a victory over Count de Grasse, and it was sold in 1867. The abbey was a quaint old mansion with Elizabethan gables and bow windows, but it was destroyed by fire in 1874, and almost rebuilt. There is a historic interest attaching to the house, for in 1642 it was the residence of Charles I., when he attacked Coventry. Soon after he had erected his standard at Nottingham, he sent word to the mayor and sheriffs to attend him there, but Coventry was strongly inclined to the Parliamentary party, and the citizens obtained possession of the magazine at Spon Tower, and they kept it for Lord Brooke, who removed it to Warwick Castle. From Birmingham four hundred men came to reinforce the inhabitants; and when Charles demanded an entrance, and was refused, some cannon were planted on Stivichall Hall to bombard the town, which, however, was done without effect. When the king heard that Lord Brooke was approaching from London with a heavy force he gave up the siege of the city and drew off his forces; and then the city was fully garrisoned by the Parliament army. When he left, the women assembled in military form, and filled up the openings and hollows in the park, that they might not any longer afford shelter to the royal troops.

Stivichall has a singular record. Mr. W. G. Fretton, F.S.A., of Coventry, writing of it, says: 'Mr. Francis Gregory stocked the whole of his estate with young oak trees, in anticipation of the future requirement of the English navy. In recognition of his patriotic example, the privilege of using supporters to his arms was granted him, and I believe this was the first, if not the only instance of a commoner being permitted this distinction. Whatever may have been his motive, the result is the beautifying of what would have been otherwise an uninteresting and dreary road across a wild common, and the formation of one of the most popular and delightful of our suburban approaches.' He is not, however, quite correct about supporters to arms belonging to country gentlemen. Of course we know that supporters are common in Scotland, even where no title is attached to a name, and a critic in

Blackwood, in reviewing Macaulay's History of England, speaks of his want of accuracy in saying that country gentlemen used to amuse themselves with discussing the armorial bearings of their neighbours, and if they contained supporters; this the critic says never was found on English armorial bearings; this is by no means so, for as a final authority has said in a heraldic book: 'There have been many, who, although they were neither ennobled nor ever enjoyed any public office under the Crown, assumed and bore supporters, which were continued to be used by their descendants, until the extinction of the family; as amongst others, the Heveninghams of Sussex, the Stawells of Somersetshire, Wallops and Titchbournes of Hants, Lutterells of Somersetshire, Pophams of Hants, Covert of Sussex, Savage of Cheshire,' etc., etc.; and he adds that these families either used such emblems on their seals, or the glass windows of their halls or churches, to show that they had a prescriptive right to use them.

Stivichall belonged to Ranulph, Earl of Chester, in the time of King Stephen, and his son Hugh conveyed the manor to Walter Durdant, the then Bishop of Coventry. It passed through various proprietorships until it came to Thomas Gregory, who died in the sixteenth of Queen Elizabeth. In 1552, Elizabeth Swillington of Stivichall gave £140 to purchase certain lands, and intended that these lands were to be expended in repairing certain roads about Coventry. The present church of Stivichall, or Styvechale as the church was sometimes called, stands on the wreck of the old one that was demolished in 1810. An old tradition says that the present edifice was erected by one James Green, a stone mason, who had no assistance at all except one labourer.

The road from Rugby to Coombe Abbey is exceedingly pleasant, and well worth a summer's walk. Within about two miles we pass the beautiful village of Newbold on Avon. It has an old church with a square tower that forms a prominent feature in the landscape. It is a pleasant village, and the church is a vicarage that includes the townships and hamlets of the Lawfords and Little Harborough and Cosford. Great Harborough, when Henry II. was king, was held by a family, Herdeberg, and the one name is derived from the other, as we so often find in old English centres; sometimes the family is named from the locality, and as often the reverse. The church, which is dedicated to All Saints, is a small edifice, and the living is put down at £298 a year.

Little Lawford is a short way to the west, and there is a good road to Coombe through it. It also has some historical records, for it was in possession of Turchil de Warwick before the Conquest, and descending to the Earls of Warwick, it was granted by Earl William to Robert de Craft, and continued in his family until the year 1441, and then it came by marriage to the possession of Thomas Boughton, a Bedfordshire squire; and his descendants remained in the mansion until the murder of Sir Theodosius Boughton, by poison, in 1788. The manor afterwards belonged to the Caldecotts.

The circumstances of the crime were these: Sir Theodosius Boughton came into possession of the estates in the later part of the eighteenth century, and his way of life was not regular; he was descended from a Bedfordshire gentleman, who inherited the estates from the family of Craft. This was in 1441, and they remained in the family until the end of Theodosius Boughton. He had an only sister who married Captain Donellan, and who thus became heir-presumptive to the property. He stayed with his brother-in-law, and noticed his irregular habits with great satisfaction; but as he continued to live, and might have had some years before him, he decided to administer poison in the form of a sleeping draught, and afterwards he accidentally let it all be known. He was tried at the Warwickshire Assizes, and executed the following spring. It is said that his courteous demeanour did not desert him even at the last, and he ascended the scaffold on polite terms with the executioner.

There are some charities connected with Newbold on Avon. The Oneley Charity provides, among other items, five shillings to be given in cakes to the children of Newbold for saying their Catechism on Palm Sundays.

From Newbold on Avon there are two roads of equal distance to Coombe Abbey; one goes by the picturesque mill of Little Lawford and King's Newnham, or Newnham Regis, so called from its having in early times been royal property. It was, however, held from the time of Henry I. to the dissolution by the canons of Kenilworth, when it was granted to John Dudley, Duke of Northumberland; but upon his attainder it reverted to the Crown. The church has for a long time

been desecrated, and the cemetery was converted into a rick-yard. The ivy-clad tower is shown here, and it is very picturesquely situated. The walls of the building were internally covered with fresco paintings, which are described by Dr. Thomas as representing the Offering of the Magi, the Descent from the Cross, and the full-length figures of the four Evangelists.

Dr. Buckland, in speaking of this place, says that in 1815 some remains of great interest were found here. There were two splendid heads of the Siberian rhinoceros, with other relics from the same class of animal; and many enormous tusks and teeth of elephants, with some stags' horns. One of the heads was presented to the Radcliffe Library at Oxford, and the other to the Geological Society of London. This road passes through Binley Common on to Binley, where there is a Grecian church built by Earl Craven in 1772; and, like all buildings in that style in England, it is sadly out of keeping with the surroundings. Formerly Binley was divided between the monks of Coombe and Coventry, but now it belongs to the Earls of Craven. This road to Coombe entails a turn upon the right hand to reach the front of the abbey, when we pass by the lower end of the great lake.

Another, and perhaps more direct route, is along Cathiron Lane, which is a charming road leading on to Brinklow. Many are the rustic scenes here. It passes by the Oxford Canal, and in one part by Hungerfield it joins it for half-a-mile. It may be remarked that this canal is a very important water connection between London and the western counties. Like the Ashby-de-la-Zouch Canal it starts from the Coventry Canal, its point of junction being Longford.

Brinklow is situated on the Roman Fosse-way, and a glance at the road from it to Bretford will illustrate how straight the Romans made their streets, quite independently of all irregularities on the surface of the earth. Not far from the churchyard there are the remains of a British camp and tumulus. These, it is

Brinklow tower.

supposed, when they came into possession of the Romans, were utilised for purposes of defence. Cannon balls have been found in the mound, and from the top there is a fine view of the surrounding country. Brinklow Tower is a good example of Tudor work, but the upper windows belong to an earlier period than the lower window which is shown. The church is situated in the middle of rustic fields, and is a very delightful summer's excursion.

From Brinklow to Coombe Abbey the road is about two miles, and many are the fine stately trees we see. The abbey is imbedded in woods, which indeed seem to flourish greatly in this part of England, and the

Brinklow to Rugby

game covers are hardly second to any in the kingdom. Part of the ancient abbey remains, and it would seem to date back to the age of Stephen, but the greater part of it has been rebuilt, and that not in a very happy style. After the dissolution the abbey lands were granted to John, Earl of Warwick. This was in the reign of Edward VI., and on his attainder they passed into the possession of Robert Kelway, whose daughter conveyed them to Lord Harrington, and his daughter, the Countess of Bedford, disposed of them to the Craven family, in whose possession they still remain. The old cloisters form part of a quadrangle, and it is in these that the old architecture remains. A range of buildings that was erected in the early part of the eighteenth century hardly suits the site, but it has some fine views of the park and the great lake. This lake covers the considerable area of ninety acres, and is supplied by a brook that runs through a branch of the Trent valley. The park itself is very fine, occupying an area of about

In Coombe Abbey Park

500 acres. The herds of deer, when kept up to the mark, number 200, and the grounds and shelters in every way serve their habits. There are covers that, until recently, abounded with game, and not a few of the almost extinct animals, such as badgers and fumarts were found on the lands. The great lake swarms with fishes, and it is said even that bitterns, now almost birds of the past, have been seen occasionally in recent days there.

Coombe Abbey is decorated throughout with costly care, and the ancient furniture is of great value, as are also the collections of arms and relics. There is a room called the Bohemian room, that is shown to visitors, and this contains the portrait, full length, of the Princess Elizabeth with her numerous family of sons and daughters.

Her name is intimately connected with the history of this part of England, as she was, though quite unblemished and innocent of the designs of Catesby and his followers, the heroine of the Gunpowder Plot. The princess was under the wardenship of Lord Harrington, and, as has been already stated, the Gunpowder conspirators, after succeeding in demolishing the king and his Houses of Parliament, intended to proclaim Elizabeth as queen, being quite certain that her youth and simplicity had prevented her from having become a too strong supporter of the Reformation, and she might be induced to be a Catholic Queen. Her beauty was great, and it is said that she was called by the cavaliers 'The Queen of Beauty' at her father's court. She was married at the early age of sixteen to the Elector Frederick, and although she was afterwards elevated to the throne of Bohemia, she lived in great want and poverty for some time. The Earl of Craven, whose ancestor purchased the estate of Coombe Abbey from the Harringtons, was, it is said, so entirely overcome with her misfortunes and her charming ways, that he joined a band of Englishmen who endeavoured to restore her husband to the throne of Bohemia. After the death of the Elector, Elizabeth returned to England and married Earl Craven, leaving him at her death a valuable collection of pictures, some of which are great ornaments to Coombe Abbey. She was buried at Westminster. There are in the Vandyck room, the drawing-room, the library, and beauty-parlour some pictures of great value, and among them portraits of Charles I. and his wife, by Vandyck; and he has the same cold, hard, and arrogant features that we see in the National Gallery in his mounted figure which came from Blenheim House, at it is said the enormous figure of £15,000. There are also many other portraits of value, but most of them are representations of the hangers-on of the House of Stuart. There are, however, excellent works of Rubens, Rembrandt, Holbein, Kneller, and others, including, it is said, Michael Angelo; and many are the art treasures and marble busts. There are very full records of Coombe Abbey in Dugdale's *Monasticon*. According to the Annals of Waverley, it was founded in 1150, but the Annals of Parcolude place the date 1149. The family of Camville granted large possessions to the abbey, consisting of the lands and woods adjoining; and these gifts were followed by many more, including some from the prior of Coventry. In this city also they had many houses and gardens granted to them by various private persons, and the grants were confirmed

by Ranulph, Earl of Chester. They also had the power to judge any one guilty of felony, if taken within their own fee, and to question any man guilty of felony, if committed even in another place; and also try him in their own court, which of course would mean the power of life and death.

Dugdale thus speaks of the final dissolution of Coombe Abbey: 'Thus in great glory, plentifully endowed, stood this monastery little less than four hundred years, till that K. H. 8, a person whose sensual disposition suited so right with that corrupt age wherein he lived, finding instruments fit for his sacrilegious purposes, contrived the destruction of it, and all the rest of those religious foundations that his ancestors and other devout persons had made; of whose subtle practices in that work, I shall, in a short corollary, before I finish this tract, make some discovery. Amongst which that general survey and valuation by commissioners from him, in 26 of his reign, at Robin Hood's pennyworths, did not a little conduce thereto, at which time this monastery, with all its revenues, over and above reprises, was certified to be worth CCCII. L. XVS. IIId. per annum. Of their hospitality to strangers, and great charity in daily relief among poor people, I need not descend to particulars. Our common historians and the traditions of such, who were eye-witnesses thereof before the fatal subversion of those houses, may sufficiently inform the world. I shall only, therefore, add what the certificate upon the before-mentioned survey takes notice of touching this abbey—viz., by their foundation, and a decree by the general chapter of their order, they bestowed in alms on Maunday Thursday every year, 4s. 8d. in money, ten quarters of rye made into bread, at 5s. the quarter, three quarters of malt made into beer at 4s. the quarter, and 300 herrings at 20d. the hundred, distributed to poor people at the gate of the monastery. Their principal officer being at that time, Thomas Howard, Duke of Norfolk, high steward, and whose fee, therefore, was V marks a year (which shows what great respect the great nobility had for those religious persons). Wm. Wilcock, Receiver General, whose fee was 6£ per annum, and Baldwin Pater, Auditor, his fee being X£ per annum.' Coombe Abbey seems to have fared much better than many others at the time of the dissolution, as the Abbot had the handsome pension of £80 a year granted to him ; and the monks fared very well. Dugdale seems to have gone very fully into the question of the merits of the dissolution of Coombe Abbey, and the effect of its dissolution on the authors of it : 'As for the causes that were usually pronounced by the founders of these religious houses, whether they have attended those violaters of what they so zealously, and with devout minds, had dedicated to God's service, I will not take upon me to say ; but sure I am, that after King Henry VIII. had accomplished this work, he thrived but little (as I shall elsewhere in particular observe). And how long shall such possessions have been enjoyed by those who had them, they that have looked into the course of this world may easily see.'

The road to Market-Harboro' lies through Leicestershire, a county that is not resorted to as it should be by English tourists. It is remarkably healthy and it occupies a high position in England, as may be gathered from the circumstance that it is a watershed which has three rivers that flow into different outlets in England. The Welland empties itself into the Wash, the Trent into the estuary of the Humber, and the beautiful Avon runs into the lower waters of the Severn on the opposite side of the county.

The geology of the county which consists of Oolite, the Cambrian system, and Trappean Rocks, together with the carboniferous and new red-sandstone age, are free from marsh or claylands, and hence its peculiar healthiness. There are just twenty-seven larger counties than Leicester, which occupies a space of 800 miles, and the county of Rutland, that covers only some hundred and fifty miles, almost nestles in it.

Leicester contains gently rising hills, and is essentially English in its character, with its quiet lanes, and old villages, and halls, and churches, that quite separate our country in its beautiful characters from all the rest of Europe. The northern range of hills is known as Kesteven Cliffe Row, and this begins near Loughborough at a place called the Six Hills; and perhaps Strathern Point, which is rather short of 500 feet in height, is the loftiest part of the range. These hills go to Belvoir park and charmingly overlook the Belvoir valley on the north-west side. The south-eastern part of the valley has ranges of hills that form a watershed between the basins of the Welland, the Wreak, and the Soar.

The roads in Leicestershire are excellent. There is the Roman Watling Street that separates Leicestershire from Warwickshire, and the Fosse Way that joins it at a place called the High Cross. To quote a brief account of the modern roads in Leicestershire, it may be said that 'the principal ones are the London and Manchester road which runs across the country from Market-Harboro' through Leicester to Castle Donnington; the Leeds or Whitehaven road from Oakham

Holy Trinity Hospital, Leice...

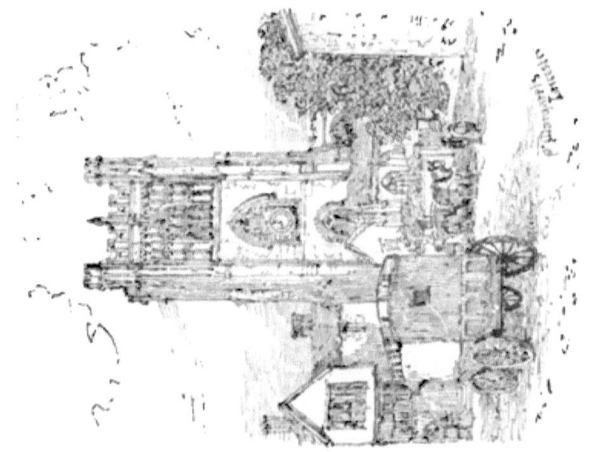

through Melton Mowbray to Nottingham; the Chester and Liverpool road from Northampton to North Kilworth, Lutterworth, Hinckley, and Atherstone. Other good roads connect Leicester with Burton, Hinckley, Lutterworth, Northampton, Coventry, and Uppingham, and there is an adequate provision of secondary roads connecting the towns and villages with each other. The total length of these roads is 1895 miles.' This is a true and fair description, and it certainly shows how we may select Leicestershire for a pedestrian's quarters.

Before the Conquest Leicester was a Bishop's see. In Henry I.'s time it was included in the diocese of Lincoln, and, in 1834, was attached to the see of Peterboro'. It is, of course, in the archbishopric of Canterbury.

In agriculture Leicestershire stands very high indeed. The greater part of the county, indeed almost all that is not otherwise occupied, is in a high state of farming. The soil is rich and the natural drainage is good. The crops which are most in vogue are those that are called green crops, but wheat, barley, and oats flourish, and when these are cultivated they yield heavy returns. But pasturage lands are now more encouraged, for the reason that expense is saved in labour, and the result is far more satisfactory and much more able to cope with foreign competition.

The breeds of Leicestershire cattle and sheep are famous, and not surpassed anywhere. The new breed of Leicester sheep is famous for the quality of the wool and for the great excellence of their flavour, and as for the cattle, we may know what they are from Stilton cheese. This cheese is so called from a small country-town in Huntingdon, where the cheese was first and is yet sold. But it is made in Leicestershire. Stilton cheeses are also made in Cheshire and in other parts of England, but none of them are quite equal to the original manufacture, though Cheshire perhaps runs it rather closely. Imitation Gorgonzola and Gruyère cheeses, we know, are made in England, and it is a sad record to make that if only the farmers would keep up to the times, no cheese would be imported, but much exported.

This slight digression may fully explain the herds of cattle that make such picturesque additions to the fields and parks of Leicestershire, and one thing will strike us as we look at them if we compare them with the cattle in old pictures: we all know Sidney Cooper's excellent works, which are nearly unrivalled, perhaps quite, among cattle painters; but Cooper's old-fashioned animals rather resemble Pharaoh's lean kine, which were so much less profitable than their better bred relatives, who ate up the fat kine, and even then they were ill-favoured and lean-fleshed, 'Such as I never saw in all the land of Egypt for leanness.' The lazy, quiet, short-horns such as we see in the Leicester fields are the farmers' best friends.

The trip to Market-Harboro' from Rugby is very delightful; perhaps it might be as well to go as far as Lilburne by train. This would seem to represent the old Roman Tripontium. Watling Street passes close by, and there is a bridge over the Avon that succeeded the Roman *pons*, probably the Tripontium alluded to, its being a three-arched bridge.

A short and pleasant walk takes us to Stanford. The church has a long chancel of three bays, and dates back principally to the early part of the fourteenth century. The chancel windows approach to tracery by the mullions intersecting at the spring of the arch. This is not a very satisfactory feature in our architecture, as the actual heads of the window-lights are out of proportion to the quadrangles that are formed above. This was soon noticed, and the tops of the lights, when a little later on cuspings came in, were filled with a separate trefoil. At Dorchester Church in Oxfordshire the windows are precisely similar in form to Stanford, but the tracery is cusped.

The church is dedicated to St. Nicholas, and it is said to have been founded by the Benedictines of Selby, a grand building on the Ouse in Yorkshire, which was converted from a monastic church to a parish church in James I.'s time, and the abbey that it belonged to was a mitred one, one of the only two north of the Trent. 'The parapet and pinnacles of the tower, although debased additions, increase the general effect. The windows are of two characters, with plain crossed tracery and rich geometrical headings.' The columns are very slender, and rise with continuous mouldings into pointed arches, and these are surrounded by a hood

of the roll-molding. 'An organ gallery intercepts the tower arch, and contains an organ once belonging to the royal palace at Whitehall, but sold by Cromwell and erected here. There is some good Perpendicular screen work under the gallery. The rood-screen was brought from Lutterworth. Furniture for the pulpit and altar, besides the covering of a large Bible and Prayer-book, were worked and given by Lady Rowe, wife of Sir Thomas Rowe, who was sent as ambassador to Constantinople in 1621. These gifts were designed as thank-offerings for the preservation of Sir Thomas and his wife in a great storm at sea, on their return from Turkey,' which it is said they left rather hurriedly in consequence of the great impression that the beauty and elegant manners of Lady Rowe made upon the Sultan. 'The history of the gift is recorded on a leaf of the Bible in contemporary writing. The church is rich in ancient stained glass and in monuments. The glass fills the east and four other windows in the chancel and some windows in the aisles, and although it has been rearranged and altered by incompetent persons, it is still of very great interest, and will amply repay study. It is chiefly decorated with smaller sections belonging to the Perpendicular and Cinquecento styles. The earliest is the east window and may date back from Edward II.'s reign. In the upper part of the window the glass remains in its original position. The lower portion is of later date, partly decorated and partly in the fine group of kneeling figures Cinquecento. These figures, as appears from arms on the tabard, represent members of the Cave family. In the other windows the glass may vary in date from about 1340 to 1360. There are various figures of holy personages and of saints. A local tradition says that all this glass was saved at the Rebellion by the parishioners who turned out in defence of their windows and prevented the destruction of them by the Roundheads. There is a sepulchral recess in the south aisle, with a mutilated recumbent figure. Nearly all the memorials of the church are for the Cave family.' This family took its name from North and South Cave in the East Riding of Yorkshire, two villages that lie just half-way between the glorious buildings of Beverley and Howden. Stanford Manor belonged to the Abbey of Selby from the Conquest to the dissolution, and in 1540 it was purchased from the Crown by Thomas Cave, the representative of the old Yorkshire family. Stanford descended to Sir Thomas Cave, Bart., and in 1839 the Barony of Braye was revived by his daughter as the representative of the first Lord Braye through her great-grandmother. It had been in abeyance from 1557 to 1839. The present Baron is the only surviving son of the late Rev. E. Wyatt-Edzell. He succeeded to the title through his mother, who was Baroness Braye in her own right. Stanford Hall is situated in a fine well-wooded deer park, and the church is in a corner of it. The hall was built about the year 1670; there was, however, an old manor-house that stood in the village of Stanford near to the church, but it has disappeared. The river Avon passes through the park, and is crossed by a picturesque bridge just at the outside. The country is well wooded, and the very land for game.

Sir Thomas Cave was the son of Sir Thomas Cave, Knt., and in 1641 he was created a baronet by Charles for services rendered to the Crown. He married a daughter of Viscount Wenman, and there is a very tragic story told of his third son, Brigadier Ambrose Cave.

He was in the Life Guards, and one of the officers of his regiment was named Biron. He had had many words with him, and Cave had always treated him with much forbearance; but one day while he was sitting in a chair Biron suddenly approached and ran his sword through the back of his body. Cave expired very shortly afterwards, and a search was at once made for the assassin; but he had disappeared and was never afterwards heard of. The river Avon runs pleasantly

Stanford Hall

along Stanford Hall, and if we cross it by the road that bounds Stanford Park, and pass what is termed Gravel Hill, we shall reach the road that passes by Swinford on to Market-Harboro'. Within a half-hour's quiet walk we reach South Kilworth, which is very apparent from the distance. The road is exceedingly pleasant and well shaded with trees, and in every direction we see rusticity itself, far away removed as it is from all manufacturing districts. The living is in the gift of the Lord Chancellor, and the spire and its surroundings form many a pleasant picture to the wayfarer. The

South Kilworth Church.

present holder of the living was a fellow of Magdalen College. The value is put down in the Church records at a gross income of £423 per annum.

South Kilworth

On Road to South Kilworth

North Kilworth is not much more than a mile from South Kilworth, and many are the beautiful prospects we have of it along the road, sometimes disappearing behind trees and soon after showing itself again a little nearer. The living is a valuable one and is in the possession of the Rev. C. W. Belgrave, who was for some time a chaplain in the Royal Navy. He served as such in H.M.S. the 'President,' and the 'Leander' at Lisbon, and afterwards in the Black Sea fleet during the Crimean War. The patron of the living is his relative Colonel Belgrave.

North Kilworth Church.

As we proceed on towards Market Harboro' we pass the beautiful country town of Husbands Bosworth. The church is a living of great value, and the rectory house which stands near is a fine residence. Bosworth is in possession of the family of Turvile who occupy Bosworth Hall. The Turviles or Tourvilles came over with William the Conqueror, and the name may still be seen on the roll at Battle Abbey. Soon after the Conquest they came into possession of great estates in the counties of Warwick and Leicester, being lords of no less than six manors. William de Tourville was companion-in-arms to William the Conqueror, and the family have had an uninterrupted succession down to the present time. William Turville was high sheriff of Leicestershire in 1433 and 1434. He succeeded to the estates of Staunton Harold, and his grandson, Sir William Turville, was appointed one of the commissioners for taking the ecclesiastical survey of the county of Leicester by Henry VIII.; and it is a curious illustration of the great power of the Crown that Henry granted him the privilege of enclosing his park at Normanton, which, without his commission, he would have been unable to do, any more than a man could embattle his dwelling without a permit from the Crown.

The road from Bosworth on to Theddingworth is finely shaded with trees that bound the park, and which, like those that formerly stood at Ashby St. Legers, are almost in profusion. The county that had Sir William Turville as an ecclesiastical commissioner had many abbeys, and the moderation of the report would almost show that Sir William stood well with the dignitaries. His descendant, and the heir to the estates, married a daughter of Sir Francis Englefield, whose ancestor had a rather conspicuous history when Sir William Turville was appointed to the commissionership. He was sheriff of Berkshire and Oxfordshire in the reigns of Henry VIII. and Edward VI. He was a chief officer in the princess Mary's household, and was sent to prison by Protector Somerset and the council as he would not prevent the hearing of Mass. But on the accession of Mary he was called in as a member of the privy council, made a master of the wards, and he obtained a grant of the manor of Fulbrook in the county of Warwick, part of the lands of the attainted Dudley, Duke of Northumberland.

Theddingworth is of great interest and beauty. It was given by the Conqueror to the Earl of Chester, Hugh Lupus, who was the ancestor of the Grosvenor

Theddingworth Church

family. The manor afterwards became the property of the Earl of Mellent, who granted it to Ralph Pincerna, or Bottler, as he was also called, from his holding the office of butler to his lordship, and the church was afterwards given to Leicester Abbey. The architecture of Theddingworth is early and very excellent. It has been 'restored,' as the modern word goes, but it is one of the very few churches that have not lost their ancient looks by being 'restored,' and we all know that 'modernising' would as a rule be a better word.

Lubbenham is a large village town two miles from Market Harboro'. Here there once stood a fine old manor-house, of which a sketch and description are still preserved. It was well gabled and supplied with mullioned windows, but it was pulled down in 1774 and the materials sold. The estate had come into possession of a younger son who never had expected it, and during the lifetime of his elder brother he built a much more imposing residence and pulled the family seat down. There is a belief that it once was a religious house, but its chief interest lies in the circumstance that it was here Charles I. spent the last night of his prosperity, the night before the battle of Naseby. There is also a house still remaining at Lubbenham where Charles lodged on the night of June 4th when on his road from Leicester to Oxford.

It is leaving our route a little, but the subject is perhaps better followed if we turn aside to Holdenby, an old residence near Althorpe Park. We should reach it through Welford, Cold Ashby, Guilsborough, Ravensthorpe and East Haddon. Some parts of this route are not quite so picturesque as others. Welford has a church of some interest, which, however, was modernised in 1872 as a memorial to the Hon. F. W. C. Villiers of Sulby Hall; a new south porch and south aisle were built. 'The north arcade of the nave is Early English, circ. 1240. The chancel is Perpendicular except the eastern bay with its window, which was allowed to remain when the rest was rebuilt, circ. 1430. Remark in the chancel the unwieldy heads serving as corbels, and the modern decorations very striking and harmonious.' The tower is very good Perpendicular work, and not far off is the Premonstratensian Abbey of Sulby. There is nothing to notice at Thornby or Cold Ashby, but Guilsborough is of interest, and here we are some six miles from Market Harboro', and four from the house where Charles was kept confined while arrangements were set on foot for his restoration to the monarchy. His old opponents were not against this, as he had promised all kinds of useful reforms and kindly treatment to his old enemies, but letters that fell into Cromwell's hands showed how untrue his promises were, and what designs he had against the supporters of the Parliament cause. At Guilsborough there is a grammar-school of some importance, that was founded by Sir John Langham in 1688. His descendant lives still at Cottesbrooke Hall. The park is a very large one, and the long straggling village bounds the south-west side. The present school is under the head-mastership of the Rev. F. W. Kingston. The church stands in a beautifully wooded dell, and belongs principally to the fourteenth century. The tower is very simple and beautiful. Ravensthorpe has a church with a very ancient tower belonging apparently to the latter end of the fourteenth century, and there is, what is so priceless now, some original seating. East Haddon has a church of much interest and charmingly situated among woods, and Long Buckby lies about two miles to the west. On one of its church bells is the inscription—

> If at my sound you don't prepare,
> You are not inclined to come to prayer.

East Haddon lies within a short distance of Holdenby Hall, where Charles was confined.

In the excellent Northamptonshire *Notes and Queries* there is a very interesting record of the way in which the high-handed cavaliers treated those opposed to them, and it is valuable as showing the disturbed state of the county in 1642, just at the beginning of the parliamentary action. This relates to a very scarce tract that belonged to the collection of George III., and the title is, ' A True Relation of the Barbarous Crueltie of divers of the bloudie Caveleers ; so especially and principally now in the County of Northampton, where they fight and kill and slay, and commit other horrible, execrable, and detestable insolences and outrages, as may be seen by the examination of divers persons taken.—Before Laurence Ball, Mayor of Northampton, Sir Richard Samwell, Clifton Catesby. Sent up to Parliament and by them commanded to be printed. John Browne, Cler. Parl. August 11, 1642.' The information, which bears the stamp of truth, says that on August 9, fourscore of troopers armed with carbines and pistols beset the house of John Hollis the elder, but the informant could not repeat what was said as the house was far distant, but he found near by, one Thomas Winckles, shot dead in the breast, and inquiring of one

Obadiah Marriot, who was there, how such a thing could have happened, he said that he heard Winckles say he was for the king and the Parliament, whereupon he was at once shot dead, and when Marriot said that they had slain a faithful subject of the king's, one of the troopers struck him several times with a sword, and when he fled away for safety, he was fired at, but, of course, in the musketry of those days the direction of a ball was erratic, and he escaped. Witnesses beyond reproach confirmed all this, and in some way it may partly illustrate the circumstance that Northamptonshire was really the beginning and the end of the Civil War.

Holdenby was one of the manors belonging to Charles, and when he was sent there after the Civil War had been ended, he was well treated, and all luxuries allowed him. His removal was in February 1647, and the lanes and highways were well lined at places by crowds, not unkindly, to see him pass. When he was surrendered by the Scotch, he was taken, with a guard of 900 horse and dragoons, to Holdenby, which was the favourite resort of his father, owing to its great hunting attractions. Indeed Charles entered Holdenby with all the state of royalty. When he was settled at his residence he wrote to the Parliament requesting that some of his chaplains might be sent to him because he wished to consult them about various matters of great import, but the Commons were too much alive to permit this, most probably knowing that he was meditating a new civil war.

The Parliamentary commissioners had their own

chaplains, and these were earnest men, and preached each week in the chapel Charles attended, but he would not let them say grace at his table—that he always did, standing up, himself. Every freedom and luxury was granted him. He used to play chess after dinner, and was especially fond of the game of bowls, which he played sometimes at Holmby, and sometimes at Althorpe, where the ground was rather better. Whyte

Remains of Holmby house.

Melville in his work *Holmby House* thus speaks of this charming county. 'The slope of the ground which declines from it on all sides offers a succession of the richest and most pastoral views. Like the rolling prairie of the far west, valley after valley of sunny meadows, dotted with oak and elms, undulates in ceaseless variety as far as the eye can reach, but, unlike the boundless prairie, deep dark copses and thick luxuriant hedgerows diversify the foreground, and blend the distance into a mass of woodland beauty.' There was a long walk in the garden here, that Charles used to enjoy, though accompanied, of course, by one or two commissioners, and this is still called the ' King's walk.'

There can be no doubt that during his stay here he was plotting another war, and secret information was conveyed to him, sometimes by Mrs. Cave of Stanford Hall, and sometimes by Major Bosville, who came disguised as a fisherman. But all this was intercepted by the commissioners, until at last he was removed from Holmby. And here there seems to be some little difference in the accounts; some say that he himself was a party to his removal. Green, in his *History of the English people*, says, 'A rumour that the king was to be removed to London, a new army raised, a new civil war begun, roused the soldiers to madness. Five hundred troopers suddenly appeared before Holmby House, where the king was residing in charge of the Parliamentary commissioners, and displaced its guards. " Where is your commission for this act ? " Charles asked the cornet who commanded them. " It is behind me," said Joyce, pointing to his soldiers. " It is written in very fine, legible characters," laughed Charles. The seizure had in fact been previously concerted between Charles and his coadjutors.'

Very high as such an authority is, there seems to be some little difficulty in seeing why Charles should be a party to his removal, unless he contemplated, in some way, a renewal of the civil war, for Holmby was the last place where he enjoyed any personal liberty. There is another account that differs slightly, but both may be correct in a measure. On June 2, 1647, the commissioners informed the Parliament that a party of horse, 700 strong, had arrived at Kingsthorpe, near Northampton, from the army on Triplow Heath, and that they proposed to seize the king. Charles was playing

Holmby.

at bowls in Althorpe Park when word was sent him that an unknown party of horse was on its way to Holmby. He at once returned, and for some reason that seems unaccountable, Colonel Graves, who was the governor of Holmby, fled away, believing that he was wanted. The troops were at Harleston when Charles was apprised of their mustering, and he had the place closed and everything made ready for a defence. At break of day, June 3, or not very long after midnight, the troops from Harleston appeared, drawn up in front of the great gates of Holmby, and the soldiers in charge of the king received them with the most cordial of welcomes. They remained quiet all the next day, and it was afterwards resolved that 'For the peace sake of the kingdom,' the king should be removed. Cornet Joyce, according to this account, went up to the king's bed-room door and demanded admittance, which Charles refused till the morning. But at six the following day, the troops were drawn up in the principal court, and Charles was removed. They reached the delightful residence of Hinchingbrooke House, now the seat of the Earl of Sandwich, but formerly belonging to the Cromwell family. The commissioners, it is said, protested, but all in vain.

When the Commonwealth was established, all the royal houses and domains were, of course, under the control of commissioners, and there was passed 'An Act for the Commons in Parliament assembled, for sale of Honours Manours and Lands heretofore belonging to the late King, Queen, and Prince,' and in January 1650, Holdenby House was sold to Adam Baynes, Esq. He had been a captain in the Parliamentary forces, and lived at Knowshop Hall, near Leeds, and he represented Leeds in the Long Parliament. He paid what in those days was the enormous sum of £22,299, and this sum included the house, the park, and mill, and 200 heads of several sorts of deer, and some wild cattle. In the conveyance, which is dated 27 January 1650, it is said that the building materials of the house available for re-using were worth £6000, over and above the cost of taking them down. But this seems to have been rather excessive, as Captain Baynes, according to a memorandum in possession of the Isham family, states that he sold the materials for £3500 and the timber for about £500. There is in Northamptonshire *Notes and Queries* a well-illustrated page showing three houses built from the materials. Now, unfortunately, they are pulled down, for the architecture is excellent.

Captain Baynes thought that his title to the property might possibly be disputed, as indeed it was pretty certain to be if the royal family were ever restored.

At the Restoration, the whole of the property was claimed by the second Charles and his commissioners, and the ruins with the title of baron were given by James II. to the French Marquis de Blanquefort. We know now that the house must have been of great splendour. It was said to have been built by John of Padua, a designer of whom we know very little. He is said to have designed Longleat and Woollaton, and some portions of Stoneyhurst College, in Lancashire, but his name is quite enshrouded in doubt and mystery, and we can see that Woollaton is the work of more than one architect. Hatton, in 1579, writes to Lord Burleigh that it was built in imitation of Theobalds, and in the same year Burleigh visited Holdenby, and as he came to the house he speaks of it as, 'Led by a large, long, straight, fair way, I found a great magnificence in the front or front pieces of the house, and so every part answering to the other, to allure liking. I found nothing of greater grace than your stately ascent from your hall to your great chamber, and when you were wont to say it was a young Theobalds, truly Theobalds I like as my own, but I confess it is no otherwise worthy in any comparison than a foil.' Sir Thomas Heneage, writing in 1583, speaks of the house: 'The best and the most considerate' that his eyes ever saw, and says it will hold the pre-eminence to all other houses he ever saw in England. Morton, who wrote a description of Northamptonshire not very long after the house was built, says of the gardens, 'Above the rest is especially to be noticed with what industry and toil of man the garden has been raised, levelled, and formed out of a most craggy and unprofitable ground, now framed a most pleasant, sweet and princely place, with divers walks, many ascendings and descendings, replenished also with many delightful trees of fruit, artificially composed arbours, and a distillery house. The house itself is a very beautiful building, erected with such uniformity and so answerably contrived, as for the quantity and quality is not to be matched in the land.' There is the fine old neglected mansion of Kirby still remaining, and it is worthy of note that by careful measurement it was found that the same templates were used for the mouldings of both houses.

MARKET HARBORO'.

To return to our route to Market Harboro'. Lubbenham lies within about a mile of it, and very charming the road is on a summer's day. Market Harboro', like other centres in this part of England, is surrounded

Entering Market Harboro from Leicester road

with old churches, and, before proceeding, we might make a few remarks on some of them. Little Bowden is to the south-east of Market Harboro', and its church tower is built of wood, though not of great antiquity.

Great Bowden is on the Leicestershire side of Market Harboro', and is well worthy of a visit. The church belongs, for the most part, to the early years of the fourteenth century, but in the fifteenth century, as at Market Harboro', the decorated piers had been cut away to make room for those of a later date. The parapet of the tower is pierced with cross-slits, such as were used in the middle ages for fortified buildings. There is a septagonal font in the church, with a large wooden cover, which would seem to belong to the Jacobean period.

Sutton Bassett lies a little farther down on the Welland valley. The chapel here is small, and unimposing in outline; 'its bell, gable, and turret being the only elements of the picturesque in its exterior.' The south and west windows are interesting, and partly to these it is owing that the church escaped demolition. The doorway is early Norman, and of great interest; and in the north side of the chancel there is a little old low side window of which there are plenty of examples round Rugby, but their use is quite a puzzle now. They were not glazed, but had a wooden shutter, and if we only consider what the plagues and pestilences were in old times, perhaps this may lead to some slight explanation. Not very long after the building of Sutton Bassett, a great pestilence swept over England, and it is estimated that within five years England had lost one-third of her inhabitants. In 1352, when Gothic architecture was in its glory, a fearful plague swept over England, which had travelled from China, where nearly a million people fell victims to it ; and it is calculated from statistics that, taking a fair average, 75,000 perished in London alone. Now it is probable, and no other explanation is so free from doubt, that those who were afflicted with the plague came to the low side window for priestly aid and ablution, and were, perhaps, borne away by their friends. This chapel is a very interesting example of Norman work, somewhat altered a century after it was built.

Weston by Welland has some picturesque old houses with mullioned windows and projecting bays, and is abundantly worthy of a visit ; but the church has been quite modernised. The church of Ashley, which lies about a mile farther east, has been to some extent modernised, but not quite so completely. A description of it in the Leicester Archæological Society's *Transactions* thus speaks of it : 'The beauty of the tower and spire excited general admiration ;' and the visitors said : 'Of all the churches they had seen, this was the most remarkable for its beauty. The tower and spire had a history if it could be gone into. There had evidently been repairs effected, and at that time the coats-of-arms, that were evidently of the fifteenth century, had been put up on the tower, which, considering how little was done, was rather unfair to the original founders.' The stilted bases of the pillars formed a remarkable feature in this church. There were specimens of the windows seen at Sutton, on each side of the chancel, and the three sedilia resembled those at Market Harboro'.

To return, however, to Market Harboro', and to

quote the account of the parish church, which the Rev. T. James read to the Leicester Archæological Society: 'The great feature of the church, as all might perceive, was the extremely beautiful tower and spire which were built on the pyramidical principle from the very basement to the apex. Every stage of the tower battered in, and there was not a singular perpendicular line about it. If they examined all the finest spires in

In Market Harboro'.

Europe, he believed they would find them formed on a similar principle. He could not agree that the window alluded to had been brought from another church; he thought that the chancel tower and spire were built in the early part of the fourteenth century, and that the same architect designed the whole. This might be inferred from the similarity of the window referred to and the fine geometrical east window, which had been so well restored. It was remarkable that in the fifteenth century they cut the whole of the nave, put in architecture of a very inferior character, and added a perpendicular clerestory. Against the tower might be seen the pitch of the lofty roof, and probably the aisles had formerly gabled roofs.

'About a quarter mile north-west of the tower of Market Harboro', some labourers digging gravel for the London Road in the beginning of July 1779, found two sculptured urns, one of a large size, and the other less by about half. The former was discovered in an inverted position, and the latter lying on one side. They were about three feet six inches under the surface. The ground above them was quite solid, but that about the smaller urn was black with fire. The contents of the larger were equal to one gallon wine measure; of the other, not more than three pints. They were formed of rough materials, and burned but slightly.' They fell to pieces on exposure to the air, but their dimensions and accurate drawings of them were taken. Nichols goes on to say that the following year two smaller urns were dug up at only a few yards' distance from the same spot; these were strongly made and well burned and stood exposure to the air thoroughly well. Other urns were discovered in the next few years, and also a pit was found three feet in diameter, and lined with stones; these bore the marks of fire, and it is probable, the same history says, that here the bodies were cremated before placing the ashes in the urns. And near the spot was also found a Roman patera in an imperfect state. 'It was of a beautiful coral colour and its material and shape would not have disgraced our Staffordshire Etruria.' This it is also said was to contain the remains of the dead, and to be enclosed in an urn after it had served funeral libations. These accounts are given by Nichols with great care, and a drawing of the urns and pateræ is carefully shown in order to confirm that Market Harboro' is not founded as the traditions, before alluded to in Nichols, state. Other Roman remains are also enumerated. No mention, however, is made of the town in Domesday Book, which is somewhat singular, if, as asserted, it really existed then.

The headquarters of Charles were here before the battle of Naseby, and here it was decided at a council of war to attack Cromwell's army, for which, Nichols says, they had a great contempt. A well where Charles watered his horse after his defeat, is still called Charles's well. The church is a fine old building that has been recently modernised; it has the unusual claim of being dedicated to St. Dionysius the Areopagite. It belongs principally to the early part of the sixteenth century, and the tower is well proportioned, as also is the beautiful broached spire. On the south side of the chancel are two sedilia that have been recently discovered. According to old traditions that are narrated in Nichols, the church was originally built by John of Gaunt, in compliance with a papal order as an atonement for some kind of irregularity, but it is now believed to have been founded by one of the Scrope family. Some parts of the church are, however, earlier than the sixteenth century, parts of it, like the tower and chancel, belong to the fourteenth. There are porches on the north and south sides, and there is a parvis over each.

There is a singular and picturesque free grammar-school near the church at Market Harboro'. It stands on three arches in the front and two at each end, and is quaintly covered with diamond-shaped oak panels, underneath is the market-place. It is called the Market Harboro' Free Grammar School, and it was built and endowed by Robert Smyth, a wealthy citizen of London. The Merchant Taylors' Company, with the accustomed liberality that has always marked them in educational matters, gave the sum of £750 to the Lord Chamberlain of London to purchase land for a schoolhouse.

TO ROCKINGHAM ON TO STAMFORD.

FROM Market Harboro' to Rockingham the distance is about nine miles, and the country is exceedingly pleasant. Between the two places lay Pipewell Abbey, that has had a very singular history, but at the time of the dissolution its revenues were very considerable, for after paying £63, 19s. for pensions to the Bishop, and Dean, and Chapter of Lincoln, there still remained an annual balance of £283.

The Abbey was built in 1143 for the Cistercian Order by William de Butevleyn, and in early days it was called in Charters, St. Mary de Devises, either because it stood on two fees, or because its demesnes lay on each side of Harper's Brook, separating the Ruthwell and Corby Hundreds. Soon after the erection of the Abbey, William Flemyng appropriated some of its resources, 'at the instigation of the Devil,' as the registers say; but he afterwards arranged to restore them on the son of the founder granting him others in exchange. The Earl of Chester was among the benefactors, and Henry de Rokeby gave the abbey his lands at Rugby. Pipewell stood in the very middle of the great forest of Rockingham.

Here Richard I. held his first great council in September 1189, and nearly all the English and Irish bishops were there, besides many abbots and priors, and some influential laymen. The vacant bishoprics were filled, and money was raised for the Crusade. Beyond this is Oakley Hall, an old building that is the seat of Sir Richard de Capell-Brooke, and beyond this the road ascends to the higher ridge of land that borders the county, and soon reaches the village and church; and here we are in the land of beauty. There is, however, a railway station at Rockingham, near the village. The castle was founded by the order of the Conqueror, in the middle of the great hunting-grounds that have left their marks to the present time. There were ironworks here from time immemorial, and it has been fancied that the castle was built to protect them. But this is not so, for it was built on ancient British foundations, and if we only examine the neighbouring grounds, we shall at once see traces of ancient handiwork. Rockingham Castle was a favourite royal residence, and the forests round it may well account for its popularity. Among its records we find that a great council was held here to discuss the recognition of Anselm as Archbishop of Canterbury. The council broke up in disorder, and the scene is famous in history. We would gladly know more of the relations of the Church and State party at the time, but the scene at Rockingham, as described by the late Dean of St. Paul's, gives us probably one of the most striking pictures we have.

Like other royal castles, Rockingham had its constables, who were either appointed for three years, or during the king's pleasure. But in 1475, or about the period when the Wars of the Roses were raging with the greatest cruelty, Edward IV. made Lord Hastings 'Constable for life.' Rockingham Castle, though it is not so complete as Warwick, has many ancient remains; some indeed are among the most ancient and interesting of any inhabited house in England. The castle within the enclosed walls occupies a space of three and a half acres; the boundary wall is nearly nine feet in thickness. The private chapel, where the conclave was held concerning the status of Anselm, is dedicated to St. Leonard, and it occupies a place over the present cellars. Anselm occupies, of course, one of the foremost places in the early history of England, and he raised up a spirit of independence in the kingdom that bore fruit in after days. The Red King did well to appoint him to Canterbury, even though his conscientious, simple, honest life procured his banishment. Henry I. recalled him, seeing how popular he was, and he continued to advance the revival of letters till his death. In his character and tone of life, he must have resembled Sir Thomas More of later days. They were distinguished beyond all other men of their age, by their learning, their utter unselfishness, and undaunted courage. Each of them followed the course he be-

Rockingham

lieved to be right, without the slightest reference to any other consideration.

But Rockingham Castle has recent associations that are of great interest to us now. It was the residence of the Marquis of Rockingham, who so often figured in the annals of Bute, and Pitt, and Fox; and it was Rockingham who joined with Pitt and the Cavendishes to support the commercial classes; and this in opposition to the selfish policy of the Bedfords and Grenvilles. Indeed, if his counsels and those of his party had been listened to, the separation of our American colonies would have taken place in a different manner, or, some think, might not have taken place at all.

The scene at Rockingham between Anselm and Rufus is well described by Eadmor, who gives us pictures of the king's advisers. The council broke up without coming to any decision, and Anselm made some sort of a submission, but with a reservation in favour of Pope Urban II., who was then at feud with the Antipope Clement III. The scene at Rockingham is described by Eadmor, and it must have been very dramatic, for we cannot forget that the two rival Popes, Urban and Clement, each wished to conciliate the powers of England, both lay and clerical.

The Edwards were often here, and doubtless the proximity of its castle to the residence of Piers Gaveston was a temptation for the visits of one of them. Often has the castle been altered and added to, but Leland's description of it as he saw it in 1545 is very graphic and true. He says, 'The castle standeth on the top of an high hill right stately, and hath a mighty ditch, and bulwarks again without the ditch. The keep is exceeding fair and strong, and in the walls be certain strong towers. The lodgings that were within the area of the castle be discovered and fall to ruine. One thing within the walls of this castle is much to be noted, that they be embattled on both sides, so that if the area of the castle were won by coming in at either of the two great gates of the castle, yet the keepers of the walls might defend the castle. I marked that there is a strong tower in the area of the castle, and from it, over a dungeon dyke, is a drawbridge to the dungeon tower.'

Part of the castle still remains since Leland's time. One of the great gates is left, and also the mound of the dungeon-keep or tower. The buildings in the first court were falling to ruins, but they soon after were restored and repaired, and they became the family residence. The massive entrance gateway is very interesting. It dates back to 1275, and has an arch flanked by two circular bastion towers. The castle as it stands has architecture of the thirteenth and sixteenth centuries. A deep chimney projects from the hall, and two early English windows have been found adjoining.

The residence is surrounded by a very heavy wall that encloses three acres and a half, and parts of this wall are three yards in thickness. The chapel of St. Leonard in which the great council was held stood between the main buildings and the keep, over the present cellars.

The estates belong to the Watson family, who have for long been lords of the manor. Sir Lewis Watson garrisoned the castle for the Crown in Charles I.'s time, and was afterwards created Baron Rockingham of Rockingham. The earldom became extinct in 1746, but the barony passed over to the last earl's cousin,

Thomas Watson Wentworth, who in 1746 was created Marquis of Rockingham. There is a curious inscription that is carved along the principal beams in the hall: 'This house shall be preserved and never will decaye, where the Almighty God is honoured and served daye by daye.' There are some very interesting and valuable pictures here by Gainsborough, Vandyck, Sir Joshua Reynolds, and others. The rebuilding of portions of the castle have been carried out by Mr. Salvin, who has had much to do with the construction of ancient country dwellings, including the splendid seat, Peckforton Castle, which was built in the second part of the present century by the first Lord Tollemache. But the outward appearance of Rockingham has not been much altered.

The village is of considerable extent and of great beauty, it ascends a steep street, and the houses are remarkably well kept and in excellent order, owing greatly to the example and care of the Watson family. There is an old house near the western entrance that at one time was the principal hostelry, such as is common to all great residences, but now it is much altered. There is a bridge over the Welland here, and at its end the counties of Rutland, Leicester, and Northampton join. These places where the counties joined used to be held in great estimation in old times for bull-baits and prize-fights, because when a justice with police appeared it was only necessary to go to the adjoining county, and indeed too often it is said the justices were among the spectators. The bridge over the Welland

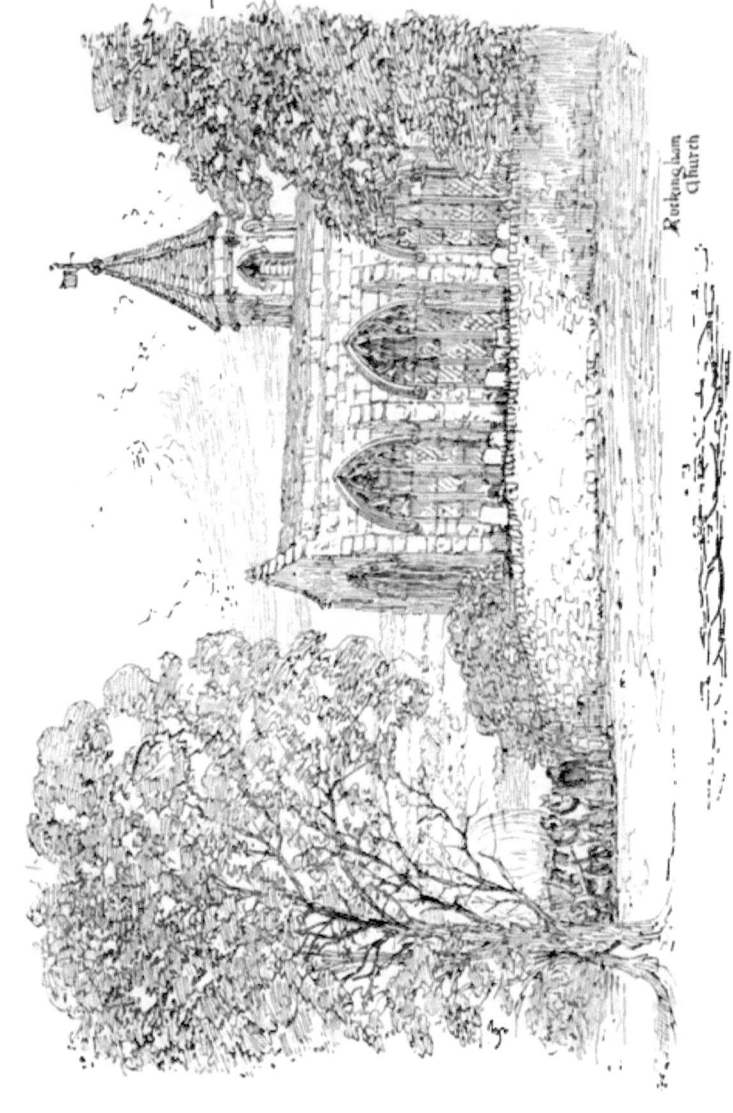

Rockingham Church

leads to the highway through Caldicott, Uppingham, and Oakham : from some parts many churches are seen.

The houses of Caldicott are built of a reddish-yellow stone which gives the village rather a gloomy appearance, yet there is more life and activity inside it than might have been expected from the exterior, and some little trade in farming produce is done. Rockingham station stands in it. The church is poor, and built almost in the latest style of Gothic. There was a fresco at one time of Adam and Eve under the tree of knowledge, but this is almost entirely obliterated. The tower is weak and slender, and the tall spire that stood on it was shattered by lightning in 1798, but has since been rebuilt. This church is a chapelry of Lyddington, and is dedicated to St. John. In the roof is the date 1648. There is one interesting feature in it, and that is the front, which is Early English. This front is square, and has chamfered edges ; it is enriched with an unusual ornament.

There used to be an old family of Caldicott living here who were of some dignity, for, in the reign of Henry VIII., John de Caldicott was twice high sheriff of the county, and his son served the same office under Elizabeth, but the Caldicotts have long since ceased as a family. There is a very pleasant approach to all this district from Uppingham, that leads through Stoke Dry to Easton Magna and Caldicott, and on all directions there are scenes of rustic beauty. Uppingham, like Rugby, cannot boast of much antiquity or picturesque beauty, though it is surrounded by charming landscapes, as indeed we may say all this part of England is. There are many roads leading here, but the road that leads from Uppingham is extremely fine, and as we pass a place called King's Hill Lodge a grand valley opens up on our right hand, which is seen through an avenue of forest trees that grow on each side of the road. Everything is in a high state of cultivation, and when farming was lucrative this must have been a most desirable place for an estate. A road across some fields will bring us in about an hour's walk to Great Easton. The spire and tower of this church are peculiarly fine and were built when Early English architecture was at its best. There are not many villages in England, if we except those near large towns, that can boast of such comfortable, substantial houses. Many of these stand in well-kept gardens, and Thackeray's beautiful description of Clavering almost applies to Great Easton. 'Looking at the little old town of Clavering St Mary's from the London Road as it runs by the lodge at Fairoaks, and seeing the rapid and shining Brawl winding down from the town and skirting the woods of Clavering Park, and the ancient tower and peaked roofs of the houses rising up among trees and old walls, behind which swells a fair background of sunshiny hills that stretch from Clavering westward, the place looks so cheery and comfortable that the traveller's heart must have yearned towards it from the coach-top, and he must have thought that it was in such a calm friendly nook he would like to shelter at the end of life's struggle.'

The road across the fields to Easton is rather dull in places, but there cannot be many poachers about if we may judge from the great numbers of partridges that spring up as we pass along it.

If we take the high road, which is a little longer, we pass through a much more beautiful country, and after turning to the left and entering the Easton Road we shall soon come to two lane-ends, the right one will bring us to the site of Bradley Priory. There is still a well left which is called the holy well, but no trace of the buildings remains. The establishment was very small, and in King John's time its revenues were only £4, 5s. 9d. per annum, and only two names besides the last prior's have been discovered, John de Querendon and John Penny, who was also Abbot of Leicester, but resigned it on becoming Bishop of Carlisle. John Owndell, the last prior, came to his slender dignities in 1509, and at the time of the dissolution the total annual value was assessed at £20, 3s. 6d., and included the lands that were the demesne of the priory. The situation in a little vale that forms a sort of close to the larger is extremely picturesque, and could we see it as it was at the dissolution we should see a very charming picture indeed.

After passing Caldicott we cross the Eye, and soon after come to a bridge of three arches that crosses the Welland. The low meadow-lands that lie between Easton and Rockingham are very delightful in summer weather. I went over them on a glorious July day and here and there were groups of cattle and sheep that seemed as if they were bent upon enjoying their brief lease of life, in their own listless way, and they were arranged often in groups so picturesque that Cooper or Ansdell though they might have copied them could never have postured them. Rockingham village lies on each side of a steep street which ends with the castle gates and the church. There is a fine old conduit here over which once stood a cross. The base of it is yet remaining. A never-ceasing spring of the clearest and most delicious water runs from it, and without pump or bucket supplies the pails of the villagers; indeed if the group I saw there had only been furnished with the panniers we see in Germany, Rockingham would have conveyed the idea of a beautiful old country town on the Rhine.

If one village is to be chosen as the most charming in this land of pleasant ones, the palm must fall to Rockingham. The street is steep and there are well-kept houses with broad charming gardens and shady trees, and there is at the western entrance of the village an old 'hostel' such as we so commonly find outside important strongholds like Rockingham Castle. It has been altered much, but retains some of its ancient character still, though it cannot compare with that near Fotheringhay. Even yet we commonly see outside great manor-houses a good inn with the armorial bearings of the lord of the manor, and on the sign-board we see the '—— Arms,' giving the hostel the family name.

The approach to Lyddington is extremely pleasant. The village is well set off with forest trees, and the houses are exceptionally fine—so fine, indeed, that they

seem almost out of place in a comparatively small
country town. Doubtless, however, it is that formerly
Lyddington was an important market-town, and even
though the houses may not, in all respects, be equal in
antiquity to the days of the prosperity of the old town,
they indicate very clearly that it did not collapse when
the market was removed to Uppingham. This, however,
was a slow process, for both places had markets at the
same time. But Uppingham was more conveniently
situated, and though the Bishop of Lincoln protested
against the market in the larger town as an infringement
of the rights of Lyddington, the superior advantages
of Uppingham finally prevailed, and the wagons and
country carts lined the church square each market-day.
The church at Lyddington is extremely interesting,
and it contains some monuments and brasses. There
is one monument to an ancestor of the Rockinghams
who died in 1530, and he was apparently the secretary
and confidante (*scribam et electum*) of the Bishop of
Lincoln, who had a palace here. That he should have
been able to acquire sufficient wealth to found the
family which rose to such power in George III.'s time
we hardly need to wonder, if we consider what vast
wealth and power the bishop of a great diocese would
hold, and then at his death Wolsey was Bishop of
Lincoln, being one of the very many 'advantages' he
held. It would hardly avail to search out the vast
possessions, with the benefices and sees from which he
drew his great revenues; a single line of *Henry VIII.*
would show; and the power he held is happily expressed

by Norfolk in that most dramatic and finished of plays (II. ii. 47):—

> 'This imperious man will work us all
> From princes into pages; all men's honours
> Lie like one lump before him, to be fashioned
> Into what pitch he please.'

Whether Wolsey lived in his palace at Lyddington, or if so, for how long, I do not know if there is anything to show; but he certainly must have passed by it often, and probably made his occasional abode there. The palace, which is built on the north side of the church, is a building of exceeding beauty. It would be a model now for any advanced architect to follow, as it has so many features of excellence. Two things are kept well in mind, the chimneys are a prominent feature and so is the roof, though in modern times it would almost seem as if we wished to keep these out of sight, at any rate we might travel through the streets of London, and if we did not know it, we should hardly suspect that the houses were furnished with either the one or the other. The great mass of masonry that a chimney consists of, if we take for an example such ones as we see at the bishop's palace, becomes warmed through, and acts like a Roman hypocaust in warming a room or a residence.

The possessions of the Bishops of Lincoln were enormous, and we may learn from the transactions between Bishop Grossteste and the Pope how independent they were. Grossteste was sorely exercised, as indeed many other Englishmen were, at the proceedings of the Pope, when the Vatican was even in its most palmy days. The Pope, among other things, used to appoint Italian priests to wealthy offices in England, and not only was Grossteste free enough of speech to condemn many of the Pope's doings, but he went to Rome to remonstrate with His Holiness, and ended by saying the Pope might take to heart some lessons he could learn from previous occupiers of the Chair. The Pope was naturally indignant, and said, 'What, shall this old dotard, whose king is my vassal, lay down rules for me!' and he ended by excommunicating the Lincoln prelate with all the circumstance of 'bell, book, and candle.' This of course was to have prevented Grossteste from taking any part in any church services or celebrations; but he astonished the see by taking no notice of the anathema, and proceeded with his duties as usual, and died eighteen years afterwards much respected by every one, and his denunciation of the excesses of the ecclesiastical orders was destined to bear good fruit among the Catholics of later years.

Some old writers speak of a castle having once stood here, but it is probable that this may have been the episcopal residence before the beautiful manor-house in the churchyard was built—a residence that would be familiar enough to the reforming bishop, but every trace of them has departed. Some maps of the last century speak of 'Snelston ruins,' and though these have for long ceased to exist, the name still remains, and is attached by some old-fashioned people to a field near Stoke Dry church.

The present remains of Lyddington Manor, though

they are very noble, formed only a small part of the episcopal palace. The Hall, and the large chamber which is attached to it, formed a part of the bishop's own apartments. Some of the stained glass yet remains, and there is the inscription, 'Dominus exaltatio mea,' and 'Delectare in Domino.' There are also the arms of Lord Chancellor Russell, who was the Bishop of Lincoln in the reign of Edward IV. In Edward III.'s reign, Lincoln was occupied by a great Nimrod, who hunted about these parts, and he had the power to inflict a fine of ten pounds on any one who hunted without his leave. The manor of Lyddington remained in the possession of the Bishops of Lincoln until the reign of Edward VI., and then the yearly rent was £69, 14s. 9d. It came in Elizabeth's time to her adviser, Lord Burleigh, and descended to his son Thomas. In the year 1602 he converted the old palace into an hospital, for a warden, twelve poor men and two women, and called it Jesus Hospital, a use it retains until the present day; and in beauty and pleasant situation it fully equals the foundations of Abingdon and Ewelme near Oxford. In the hall there is a large folio Bible with an inscription in which it is called 'Lyddington Hospital Bible.' This book was given by John Clare, who was steward to the Earls of Exeter; and it has a MS. prayer inside which is always read by the warden, along with the others, at the church service. The *Gentleman's Magazine* for 1796 contains a view of Lyddington Hospital, and a careful account of the foundation and early history, and there is a copperplate engraving of it, which is geometrical, and characteristic of the art of the age.

When at Lyddington a road to Oakham would take us past the villages of Wing and Manton. Wing, or Wenge, as it is sometimes called, is an extensive

scattered village, and though it is not mentioned in Domesday-book it had an existence, and it was granted to the family of Montfort, whose ancestor, Hugh de Montfort, came over with William the Conqueror. He seems to have been a man of eminence and consideration, and was appointed coadjutor with William Fitz-Osborne, and Odo, Bishop of Bayeux, for the administration of justice throughout England. He lost his life in a single combat with Walchelm de Ferrars, but the manor descended to his posterity. Robert de Montfort, in the reign of Henry II., granted a moiety of the church in the parish to the monks of Thorney Abbey in Cambridge. He was succeeded by his brother who absolutely refused to confirm his gift, and refused to pay the abbot a legacy his brother had left.

A complaint was made to King Stephen, who commissioned the Bishop of Lincoln and the Earl of Warwick to force him to comply with the bequests of his brother, and he was obliged to submit, granting the monks of Thorney Abbey a new charter conferring on them a moiety of the church. And the mill—the mill was an ancestor of the quaint old peg-mill which forms a picturesque feature of the landscape. This was the old form of windmill that turned bodily round to let its sails catch the wind. Shortly after this, the monks got all the manor in their hands, and John de Stuteville, who possessed the other half of the town of Wenge, gave it up to the abbey. The history is interesting, as some of the abbot's successors granted a lease of ninety-nine years to the Lacy family at a rental of ten pounds per annum, and it remained in their hands until the dissolution, when it was seized by the Crown. The village stands on a hill, and has a very pleasing appearance from the surrounding country.

From Manton to Oakham the road is short, and we see the grand woods of Burleigh Park as we travel along it. Oakham is a large, straggling country town, and the road from the station does not show it to advantage, but there are many picturesque scenes in it that would well repay a long journey. The church is seen at considerable distances, and often groups pleasantly

Wing Mill
Rutland

with the town buildings. The advowson was given by Edward VI. to Nicholas Ridley, Lord Bishop of London, and his successors, but was granted to the Earl of Winchilsea in the last century.

A circumstance in the history of Oakham will illustrate curiously how landed property was held, and the penalties for trespass after game. Henry II. granted the manor of Oakham to one of the family of Ferrars, and he accompanied Richard I. to the Holy Land, but he died before the walls of Acre, during the siege that has given the theme to so much romance. It was royal property before. The manor was held by the service of one knight's fee and a half. Now the forest of Leafield

Oakham
Rutland

was not included in the liberties of Ferrars, and unluckily he trespassed in pursuit of venison into its limits. The exact amount of fines was hardly statutory in those days, and much would depend upon the circumstances of the delinquent. But he was fined 100 marks, and not only so, was compelled to pay it, about seventeen years before he met with his death in Palestine. The manor passed through many hands, but it may not be generally known that at one time it belonged to Thomas

Cromwell, who is said by Camden to have been Baron of Oakham, and Dugdale repeats the statement, which, as it seems, is accurate, though he was better known by the title of Baron Wimbledon in his lifetime. Until Green wrote his *History of the English People*, not much was known of Thomas Cromwell. Indeed he passed for a rather clever, able servant for whom Wolsey had no longer employment, in most of our school histories, but, in truth, he was certainly the ablest, and perhaps the least scrupulous, minister that ever served an English monarch. Nobody else could have dissolved the monasteries as he did, but he simply chronicled out, from period to period, the list of those that were doomed, and the fate that awaited the abbots.

Yet it was recorded of him that he was deeply attached to Wolsey, his old master, and so rapid was his rise that he was able to screen his former master from attainder. Wolsey had soon seen the power of Cromwell, and it is probable that he owed much of his overwhelming fortunes to his genius. Yet the leave-taking, as related by Shakespeare, is very human and pathetic, and nothing can be more certain than that the historical plays of Shakespeare rank amongst the accurate records of history :—

> *Wol.* 'Go, get thee from me, Cromwell ;
> I am a poor fallen man, unworthy now
> To be thy lord and master. . . .
> *Crom.* O my lord,
> Must I, then, leave you ? must I needs forego
> So good, so noble, and so true a master ?'
> *Henry VIII.*, III. ii. 413.

Green, in his *History of England*, says: 'In the whole line of English statesmen there is no one of whom we would so willingly know so much, no one of whom we know so little, as of Thomas Cromwell.' Yet as the castle must have been his residence, and Oakham was his title, one is almost disposed to think that there must be some records in the Rutland town that would prove of deep interest. For though the great chancellor was brought to the block at Tower Hill, the lands of Oakham were conveyed to his son, and in his line they were continued for three generations. It is said that, at the close of the seventeenth century, considerable remains of the old castle were standing where Cromwell must have often resided, but now all that remains is the hall. There are large and small horse-shoes in it of all dates, and in every kind of smith-craft, which are interesting to the curious, and some of them have really a sort of historical interest about them. There is a total obscurity about the origin of these horse-shoes, but the law or custom was that any baron passing through the town was obliged to leave a horse's shoe behind him. This is supposed to have some occult reference to the ancient arms of the Ferrars, but most probably it is only another form of poll-tax. In Lancashire, for example, at the country town of Ormskirk, a tax of twopence is, or till very recent years was, imposed on all four-footed animals that came to the fair, and Lord Derby's agents had barriers erected with toll-collectors. The Ferrars, in fact, were only connected with Oakham for so short a time that such a custom must have had an older and broader origin; most probably it denotes some sort of service, and in later times the service was generally paid, not by a horse's shoe, but ancient coin; perhaps the expression that was formerly applied to a new apprentice 'paying footing,' may have some connection with some such custom. At Oakham is a strange old mansion that is quite worth a pilgrimage to see, it is called Flore's House, and is only inferior in interest as a residence to the Jew's house at Lincoln. It was at first Early English, but it was much altered in the fifteenth century. The house was originally in the form of three sides to a quadrangle, and the doorway, which belongs to the thirteenth century, is still standing, and indeed is of great value. In the passage there is a very singular drain that projects from the walls, and is ornamented. 'The slat is sunk on all four sides to the centre, where there is a human head in relief, and four holes for carrying off the water;' and at the point of the arch is a staple for suspending a chained dish. Roger Flore, whose name is chiefly connected with the house, died in 1483. His estate is described in his will, and it forms a still further illustration of old times and customs. There were in his possession ten messuages, but we cannot well estimate the value of these, for no record of their size is left. Then he had a hundred acres of land, ten acres of meadow, and all their appurtenances, held of the lord of the manor by fealty only. He bequeaths his body to the parish church, and his best animal, or palfrey, to the vicar for a 'mortuary,' and we are almost reminded of conscience-money that we see acknowledged by the Chancellor of the Exchequer for short-paid income-tax in the *Times*, though, in his case, it was a genuine giant. A belief, which we would hope was a heresy, prevails that these conscientious acknowledgments in the *Times* are only suggestions by the chancellor of the period, and, indeed, that in some cases the initials indicate men known in the money world. But Roger Flore gave shillings for 'forgotten tythes.' Very few houses are left in England that can compare in antiquity with this. In York there are a few remains of value, and at Lincoln and Stamford there are also some, but in Chester there are none. In the market-place is the celebrated Butter Cross, though why this particular cross should be called a 'butter cross' is not very apparent, yet the same name lingers round all old crosses, such as Winchester, or Salisbury, or Malmesbury. It, of course, separates them from the other crosses, such as the memorial ones of Queen Eleanor, of which only three remain out of twelve, or preaching crosses like that at Blackfriars', Hereford, or the more beautiful one of Iron Acton in Gloucestershire. The cross at Oakham, or rather the two crosses, are almost unique; one has been pulled down and rebuilt recently; the octagonal one is supported by a great stone column in the centre, in which the rafters rest. Nearly everything is oak about it, and, of course, we know that Oakham derived its name from the oak, when that tree was flourishing in those parts. Those who are interested in following the tenures of property would be greatly interested in reading the astonishing changes that Oakham was subject to. It reverted to the Crown between the reigns of Henry III. and Edward III. no less than three times, and was regranted to whomsoever the king of the period desired, and though the precise dates are not now available, this must have occupied a space of not more than 150 years. At one time the manor belonged to the widow of the worthless Piers Gaveston, who, one seems to think, would have been a fitting comrade for '*Steenie*,' the Duke of Buckingham, that once held the neighbouring manor of Burley-on-the-Hill.

The celebrity of Oakham, as the guide-books say, was the notable dwarf, Jeffrey Hudson, who occupied the dubious honour of being dwarf to the selfish Queen, Henrietta Maria. One almost wonders at the straits the upper classes were put to for amusement in those days, and the slender resources they had in themselves. The fools, as we see in Shakespeare, were really the wits of a family. This Hudson figures in Scott's *Peveril of the Peak*, and Fuller in his *Worthies* alludes to him as the smallest man in the smallest county of England. Yet it is recorded that his father was a fine powerful man. He was granted two tall footmen to wait upon him when in the distinguished position he held as 'dwarf to the queen;' and he seems to have made a profound sensation by breaking through the crust of a large pie, and showing himself to the delighted audience as he skipped out on the table. He appears to have been suspected of some connection with the Gunpowder Plot, and was imprisoned. But it is an actual fact that his portrait has been painted by Vandyck, as in attendance on the queen, and the picture yet remains in possession of the Earl of Portarlington. We have, it is true, got over the taste for possessing dwarfs or jesters, but still any *lusus naturae* is a valuable possession to the owner who will exhibit it.

The town is large and somewhat straggling, but it is very pleasant, and many are the scenes of beauty that we find in it. Some of the bye-streets even have grass growing in them, but on market-days the pleasant old place is full of quaint country carts, and farmers, and gamekeepers, and—a paradise for artists.

On the outskirts of Oakham is the hospital of St. John, founded about 1390 by William Dalby, a merchant of Exton. His daughter and heiress married Roger Flore of Oakham, Esq. His descendant Roger made great alterations and additions to Flore's house, and died in 1483.

Every one who has been to Manton will have noticed the grand prospect that opens out as we look past Oakham. The spire of All Saints is very visible, and Burleigh rises grandly up on a well-wooded hill. There are, indeed, few mansions in all England so magnificently situated. The park, which is enclosed, covers an area of a thousand acres, and is full of landscapes of great beauty. Elms and oaks that have not been warped by sea breezes seem as if they were part of the ancient forests that covered these parts, so free and easy is their growth, and they look so stately that they seem as if they were to the manner born.

Mr. Wright tells us that when Villiers, the 'Steenie' of James I., purchased it, he made it one of the finest seats in England, superior even to Belvoir, and here it was that the worthless favourite entertained James in a perfectly royal manner; and it is a curious circumstance that some of the sermons that were preached before the king on the occasion of the visit are still preserved. They are by Bishop Andrewes.

Stamford lies to the east of Oakham, and is a town that is not nearly so much known by the admirers of old England as it should be; there are churches not only of antique beauty, but some of them figure in the works on English architecture as the best of existing models. Indeed I can hardly call to mind any work that has not an illustration of St. Mary's as the most perfect example of an early spire known, but the spire seems to be a little later than the tower. It is delightfully situated on the Welland, and half of it lies in Northampton while the other half is in Lincolnshire. That which lies in Northampton belonged to the Abbots of Peterborough. They held it by a baronial tenure, and it is even yet known by the name of Stamford Baron. The portion that lay in Lincoln is the 'burgh,' and was once a royal one. It is one of the five 'burghs' that, under Danish rule, had special rights and privileges, the others being Lincoln, Leicester, Nottingham, and Derby. Edmund Ironside when in difficulty with the Danes granted this, but in 944 he retook the towns and they all remained in the hands of England until the invasion of Sweyne, the king of Denmark, in

1013. The bridge that crosses over the Welland is exceedingly pleasant, and very picturesque are the views from it. It probably occupies the site of the ford from which Stamford takes its name. It lies on what is called the Great North Road that is connected with Ermyn Street and is the highway to Yorkshire from London. Dickens in *Nickleby* describes a drive on a winter's night in a mail coach, when Nicholas and Squeers were going to Dotheboys Hall with some unhappy youths: 'The night and the snow came on together, and miserable enough they were.' Then he graphically describes the fast-falling snow, and says, speaking of Stamford as the mail coach rolled through it: 'The streets of Stamford were deserted as they passed through the town, and its old churches rose dark and frowning from the whitened ground.' Many of the English sovereigns stopped here. King John has left his unhappy record in the town, and all the Edwards stayed here. When Edward lost his wife Eleanor, to whom he was so much devoted, Stamford was one of the places where his Queen's remains rested for the night, and one of the notable Eleanor crosses was erected here. Three only of these are left, but they are simply models of beauty; the other nine were destroyed during the civil war which Charles brought on. Those at Northampton and Waltham, which happily have survived the ruin, partly resemble each other, but Geddington differs widely and it is clearly the work of a different hand; still the details on it are very beautiful, and Geddington is within easy reach of Rugby. Sometimes one hopes that these models of beauty may not all be lost, but that some may have the same happy luck which fell to the writer, who one day in an ancient rockery discovered the remains of the historical Cross of Chester, about two miles from the city.

Henry VIII., Elizabeth, James I., and Charles I., also visited Stamford, and Charles I. fled here in the dis-

guise of a servant in May 1646. On his escape from Hampton Court he was received in the house of Alderman Wolph. William III., George IV., and Queen Victoria also visited Stamford, but perhaps Burleigh was more connected with some of the visits than the town itself. In 1401 the manor of Burleigh belonged to

Gervase Wykes who was chief magistrate of Stamford; it afterwards came into the possession of his nephew who was the vicar of All Saints; he bequeathed it to his cousin Margaret Chambers, and she sold it to Richard Cecil. The manor of little Burleigh was owned by the Lord Chancellor, Michael de la Pole, but as he was attainted and condemned to death in Richard II.'s reign it reverted to the crown, and eventually it was purchased by Richard Cecil, and his son William, Lord High Treasurer of England, built the palatial residence ' on the foundations of the old house that had descended to him from his father.'

Among the family pictures at Burleigh is one by Sir Thomas Lawrence known as the 'Cottager's Daughter,' and its history is very romantic. When Henry Cecil, who afterwards became the Earl of Exeter, was a minor, he married the comely Emma Vernon, from whom he was divorced; and besides that, he lost his money by gambling. His uncle was the Earl of Exeter, and he advised his retirement to the country. Cecil retired to a country farm-house in Shropshire that was rented by Farmer Hoggins, and here he resided for two years. This farmer had a daughter of great beauty and quiet natural gifts, that made Cecil compare her with others that he had met in the circles of fashion, and he married her in 1791. When the Earl died she was quite unconscious of the fact that she was a countess, and according to report they went together simply looking at the grand residences they passed, but she thought of the cottage that her husband had promised her, little dreaming of her future. The beautiful ballad that Tennyson wrote is one of his best-known works :—

> 'So she goes by him attended,
>   Hears him lovingly converse,
> Sees whatever fair and splendid
>   Lay betwixt his home and hers ;
> Parks with oak and chestnut shady,
>   Parks and order'd gardens great,
> Ancient homes of lord and lady,
>   Built for pleasure and for state.
> All he shows her makes him dearer,
>   Evermore she seems to gaze
> On that cottage growing nearer,
>   Where they twain will spend their days.
> O but she will love him truly !
>   He shall have a cheerful home ;
> She will order all things duly,
>   When beneath his roof they come.
> Thus her heart rejoices greatly,
>   Till a gateway she discerns
> With armorial bearings stately,
>   And beneath the gate she turns ;
> Sees a mansion more majestic
>   Than all those she saw before.
>
> .   .   .   .   .
>
> While he treads with footsteps firmer,
>   Leading on from hall to hall.
> And, while now she wonders blindly,
>   Nor the meaning can divine,
> Proudly turns he round and kindly,
>   "All of this is mine and thine."'

There is at the end of St. Martin's long street an entrance to Burleigh House, which, of course, is one of the historical residences in the kingdom, and like Eaton near Chester the public are kindly admitted to see the noble mansion, and the lower parts of the park are

always open to the public. Burleigh at the time of the
Conquest belonged to the Abbey of Peterborough, but
in the Domesday Survey it seems to have been held by
Geoffrey of Winchester. It soon, however, returned to
its former owners, but at about the first year of Henry
VIII. it was purchased by Cecil, the father of the Lord
Treasurer; still there was a monastic cell belonging to
Peterborough, but all rights of ownership soon came to
Richard Cecil and his son. The eldest son of the Lord
Treasurer was created Earl of Exeter in 1605; the
Marquisate dates from 1801. The house was built by
Lord Burleigh in 1575, and the earliest date that is
seen on any part of the building is 1577.

Fergusson, in his excellent history of architecture,
alludes to Burleigh as being not a very beautiful
building either in general effect or in detail, but this is
owing to the great prejudice that, when he wrote, existed against all Elizabethan architecture, so much so,
that one authority speaking of Elizabethan architecture
in a well-known book of reference, says that if there
were an Elizabethan building belonging to his family
he would not have it destroyed any more than he would
wish to see the extermination of a cripple in his family.
This is hardly fair, for the Elizabethan architecture
suits our woodlands and parks and our towns very much
more than the exotic productions of Athens. Then
the noble bay windows in the mansion that front the
outside of the building point to a feeling of security and
happiness that in those days had not commenced on
the continent of Europe, where the outsides of baronial

mansions were castellated to repel invaders, for all Europe was a troubled sea that could not rest, and the entertaining rooms of a castle faced the quadrangle of the court. The house of Burleigh is built round a court and is of Barnack stone. The Barnack quarries are now unworked, but doubtless buildingstone is not exhausted. The monasteries of Peterborough, Thorney, Ramsey, Crowland and others, were built from them, and the sharpness of the carvings is still a great feature. The tower of Barnack is a very interesting example of early work. It has long and short work at the angles, and narrow square-edged bands of stone project from all four walls at intervals. A plain string-course divides the walls about mid-way, and there are the traces of a circular sun-dial such as we see at Earl's Barton, a Northampton church that is, of course, well known all over England. The discussion as to the dates of the churches of Saxon and Norman origin, of which these have formed texts, must soon be renewed, as so great an authority as Rickman has drawn the line quite too finely. He drew, as it always seemed, a too sharp division between the Norman architecture of England and the Saxon, and some of the finest Norman buildings in England, as they are recorded in works have, it is now certainly established, a record that dates back to Saxon times. But perhaps this subject might be, and indeed will be soon, fully discussed. 'The tower of Barnack,' an excellent authority says, 'is supposed to be Saxon, but Sir Hervey Dryden, from the convoluted ornaments on the small window on the south side, and from the carvings on the upright stones, believes it to be of Danish workmanship,' and here indeed a new feature is beginning to open in our architecture.

Burleigh House is built in the form of a parallelogram round a central court, and Sir Horace Walpole said, 'The inside court struck me with admiration and reverence.' The west front is a noble example of Elizabethan architecture. The interior of the house, which is free to visitors, is a splendid example of an old palatial residence, perhaps too large, as very probably a future age would say, for human requirements where only a family is concerned. The pictures belong, for the most part, to the later Italian school that is not very much in favour now, but there are many excellent works besides. Burleigh House contains the great number of 145 rooms. The banqueting-hall is very magnificent, with its open roof and carved pendants. The chapel is reached by a vaulted staircase, and it is decorated with carvings by Grinling Gibbons, and as this is so often repeated in houses of his age, it may be well to say that the carvings are not always his, but under his guidance, and, perhaps, finishing-touch. Burleigh is finely furnished with royal furniture, and many are the beds on which it is said royalty rested, as indeed the houses that claim in the districts round Rugby that Charles slept before and after his battles; so I think we may very fairly say, in the matchless language of Henry IV. when he speaks of sleep—

> 'How have I frighted thee
> That thou no more wilt weigh my eyelids down
> And steep my senses in forgetfulness?
> And hushed with buzzing night-flies to thy slumber,
> Than in the perfumed chambers of the great,
> Under the canopies of costly state?
> O, thou dull god, why liest thou with the vile
> In loathsome beds, and leav'st the kingly couch
> A watch-case or a common 'larum bell?'

Now there really are so many claimants to houses where Charles slept before and after his battles that this would seem to be a fair answer to all.

The ceilings of Burleigh are in many instances adorned by saints from the brushes of Verrio and Laguerre, like so many of the great residences in the south.

The name of these artists is, of course, well known, and we can easily point out their work in the great mansions they were commissioned to embellish. There was a princely residence named Canons, where the Dukes of Chandos used to live, that lies on the road from Rugby to London, but is not many miles away from the latter, and here the foreign artists seem to have expended their best talents. Pope thus speaks of it in his moral essays:—

> 'And now the chapel's silver bell you hear,
> That summons you to all the pride of prayer,
> Light quirks of music broken and uneven,
> Make the soul dance upon a jig to heaven.
> On painted ceilings you devoutly stare,
> Where sprawl the saints of Verrio and Laguerre
> Or gilded clouds in fair expansion lie,
> And bring all Paradise before your eye.'

Greatly did Pope afterwards regret his notice of Canons, of which this is an extract, for the Duke of Chandos was an excellent and amiable man, and Pope even went so far as to say that he was alluding to another palatial residence, but no—his allusions were too clear, and he was not forgiven.

The collection of paintings at Burleigh numbers over 700, and contains some really very fine ones. A good authority has said, 'There is no other seat which affords so complete, and on so grand a scale, a view of the taste in arts which prevailed among the English nobility from the middle of the seventeenth to about the end of the eighteenth century.' This is perhaps true, but he omits to say that art was imported from the Continent, as indeed almost a veto had been placed on English art. The pictures we see at the time alluded to are from second-class Italian artists, and, though fairly good, are not equal to what we might acquire at any public exhibition of pictures, with indeed some fine exceptions. And I may fairly bring in the description Thackeray gave of so many houses that the wealthy built, though it is extreme. 'The house is in full view of the lake all the way, except where intercepted by the trees in the miserable island on the lake—an enormous red brick mansion, square, vast, and dingy. It is flanked by four stone towers with weather-cocks. In the midst of this grand façade is a large Ionic portico, approached by a vast, lonely, ghostly staircase. Rows of black windows framed in stone stretch on either side, right and left—three storeys and eighteen windows of a row. You may see a picture of the palace and staircase in the views of England and Wales, with four carved and gilt carriages waiting in the gravel walk, and several parties of ladies and gentlemen in wigs and hoops, dotting the fatiguing lines of stairs.' This is the satiric description Thackeray gave of one of the revival houses of England, perhaps too severe, but not indeed quite without truth, and there is, perhaps, a slight under-current in Tennyson's beautiful ballad when he speaks of what the overwhelming feeling was when the new countess saw the gorgeous paintings at Burleigh:—

> 'Faint she grew, and ever fainter,
> As she murmured, "O that he
> Were once more that landscape painter
> Which did win my heart from me."'

Burleigh House is finely wooded, and there is a large lake in the park. The avenues are very fine and extensive, and there are very grand trees of Spanish chestnut, elms, and oaks, and limes. The elm avenue, which we enter from Stamford, is very fine, and the branches of the trees are knitted and twisted in an extremely picturesque fashion. Happily strangers are allowed, on very easy terms, to visit the grand mansion, and there are among the pictures not a few that are very well worthy of notice. In the billiard-room there are seven portraits of Kneller's, and there is a head that is reported, perhaps justly, to be by Rembrandt. There is a Virgin and Child ascribed to Albert Durer, and also a Venus and Cupid which is said to be the work of Michael Angelo. The great staircase has some works of Verrio's which are said to be his best; but there is a singular Burleigh tradition about one of the figures which is said to represent the cook. Verrio was very particular about his dinner, and on one occasion the cook would seem to have neglected his tastes, and his portrait was placed among the sufferers in the Inferno, where it still remains.

When James I. came from Scotland to assume the English crown, he stayed at Burleigh, and was entertained with great magnificence. 'The house seemed so rich as if it had been furnished at the charge of an emperor. All the offices of the house were set open, that every man might have free access to buttery, pantries, kitchen, to eat and drink at their pleasure.'

On the night of the 23rd July 1643, Cromwell, with 3000 of his warriors, arrived at Stamford, and at once advanced upon Burleigh House, then occupied by a cavalier force composed of Noel, Viscount Campden's troop of horse and 300 foot, which had been annoying the Parliamentarians under Colonel Palgrave in the neighbourhood of Peterborough. At daylight, next morning, the besiegers opened fire upon the house from fourteen pieces of ordnance, but the place was found too strong for their shot, and after three hours of cannonading they sounded a parley, and offered terms. The Royalists declared they would neither take nor give quarter. A hot musketry fire was directed against the defenders, and in the middle of the day they surrendered. Oliver was magnanimous and generous,—instead of sacking the mansion, he presented the widowed countess with his portrait, which is shown in the collection.

The sixteenth century has been termed the era of palaces, and they were generally erected by high officers of state who had a convenient control over national funds. Burleigh owes its origin to William Cecil. 'My house of Burghley,' wrote Cecil in 1585, 'is of my mother's inheritance. I have set my walls on the old foundations, and yet one side remaineth as my father left it me.' There are several dates about the present building that point out the Lord Treasurer's time. Near one of the entrances within the central court is the inscription, W. Dau. de Burghley, 1577, and beneath a turret is the date 1585, and the present grand entrance was built in 1587.

William, Lord Burleigh, was the successor to Sir Christopher Hatton, for whom the memorable letter of Elizabeth was written to the Bishop of Ely when he objected to give up Ely House, in London, that Christopher Hatton desired for a town residence.

'Proud Prelate,—You know what you were before I made you what you are ; if you do not immediately comply with my request, by G—d I will unfrock you.
'ELIZABETH.'

The sagacity which chose Burleigh and Walsingham, says Green in his History, was just as unerring as that which chose the meanest of her agents, and the minister on whom Elizabeth principally relied was Cecil, and even he trembled for her success against all the great forces of France and Spain. It was in

1598 that the manor was inherited by his eldest son, Lord Burleigh the second, who was made a knight of the garter by Elizabeth, and elevated to the title of Earl of Exeter by James I. Sir Robert Cecil, the second son of the Lord Treasurer, was created Earl of Salisbury, a title that has since been raised to a marquisate. The architect for Burleigh was John Thorpe, who, in his time, built more houses than any one in England. There is a singular tale about this eccentric man among the architectural relics. He often spoke of his tomb and the monument it should support, and in a severe illness he asked a friend to write his epitaph, which was to be very short and to rhyme. This his friend managed to do in two lines of three words each. But, short as this was, Sir John Thorpe said it was too long, and faintly taking the pencil he wrote the memorable couplet of 'Thorpe's—corpse.'

If we travel about a mile south-west we arrive at Wothorpe, where there is a noble old ruin,—the ivy-clad remains of a fine old turreted mansion, which was built by the first Earl of Exeter about the year 1600, who said that 'He built it only to retire out of the dust when his great house at Burleigh was a-sweeping.' Easton lies close to, and it is the highest point in the neighbourhood, and from the tower of Easton Church, Ely Cathedral and Boston Tower may be seen on a clear day. The interior of the church is more ancient than the exterior, which dates back to the sixteenth century.

The celebrated antiquarian, Dr. Stukeley, lived at Stamford. He was an M.D., an F.R.S., and F.C.P. He was appointed to the vicarage of All Saints, Stamford, in 1729, and held the living until 1747, when he became rector of St. George's, Queen's Square, London. He bought Mr. Wolfe's house, and, writing of this in 1744, he says, 'The great gate in the town wall for the passage of waggons into the farm-yard I built up in the present form, leaving only the door; this opens into the fields. By it is a pond in that part of the town ditch, called to this day Wolfe's pond.' Dr. Stukeley founded the Brazenose Society at Stamford, which he said was 'designed to inquire into the antiquities of the kingdom, make discoveries in natural history, and improvements in the arts and sciences generally.' But the town and all the district are full of interest for the antiquarian, the historian, and the architect.

BILTON

BILTON lies a little more than a mile to the south-west of Rugby, and is reached along a pleasant road. When we arrive there we shall find two roads: one is a continuation of the Rugby Road, and it leads to what is called Dunsmore Heath, where a route or high ground through many shady trees takes us on to Coventry, passing the Roman Fosse before it reaches Ryton on Dunsmore and the valley of the Avon.

The village is a neat, pleasant, scattered one, and a charming resort on any summer's day, but, of course, the great attraction is Bilton Hall, which is so long identified with the name of Addison. He had passed a varied life, but was enabled by his ability to save enough money to purchase the hall and lands for £10,000, before his marriage with the Countess of Warwick. This he did in 1711 from the proprietor, William Boughton, Esq., of Lawford, and here he lived for the comparatively short period that preceded his death.

Bilton Hall is a spacious but picturesquely-irregular mansion, and the front that is shown is an excellent example of English architecture of the first part of the seventeenth century. The date of its erection, 1623, still remains on the entrance, incised in stone.

The gables are beautifully proportioned, and the tall chimneys give the front a fine architectural appearance.

The garden front has been altered considerably, having, in fact, been rebuilt in 1831 by the Hon. John Bridgman Simpson. Here we may see a most excellent example of what is termed the 'Dutch Gardens,' or the formal method of laying out grounds that would seem

to have been imported during the reign of the real 'William the Conqueror,' as William III. is now sometimes called. These consisted of long straight walks with yew-trees clipped into form, only too often fantastic, and representing peacocks or warriors, as I have sometimes seen, or other eccentric devices. But if these gardens are well kept, as those at Bilton are, they are always agreeable and pleasant to wander in, and it may not be out of place to say that the rules of Kemp and Loudon differ entirely in their arrangements, as their especial maxim was to let no end of any road be seen, but turn it round, and so plant some evergreen that its direction cannot be distinguished. There is a long walk that is still called Addison's Walk, and here, and in a summer-house at the end, he spent some of his most happy days. There is an avenue of elms that leads to the entrance of the old mansion, and very picturesque these are in their formations; some have been removed, but there are very good ones left.

The life of Addison and the great effect that he had and still has upon the literature of England has often been discussed and written about, and a short epitome would show how this was developed in his lifetime. If not a profound scholar, he was a very accomplished one. Macaulay says, in his usual style, that 'his knowledge of Greek, though doubtless such as was in his time thought respectable at Oxford, was evidently less than that which many lads now carry away every year from Eton and Rugby.' He was not, of course, such a scholar as Bentley, or as the professors of Greek now, but he had a very excellent appreciation of the Greek poets and writers, and many allusions to them in his works show that his knowledge was extensive and intelligent, and we all are willing to grant one of his latest requests when he wrote: 'It was said of Socrates that he brought philosophy down from Heaven to inhabit among men; and I shall be ambitious to have it said of me that I have brought philosophy out of closets and libraries, schools and colleges, to dwell at clubs and assemblies, at tea-tables and coffee-houses.' This really is a pithy analysis of the *Spectator*.

Addison was born on May 1, 1672, or just in the middle of the reign of Charles II. His father was the rector of Milston, near the charming old country town of Amesbury, which is situated on the Upper Avon, some two miles distant from Salisbury Plain. The church was once portion of an abbey, and any one who has passed through the dreary wastes of the plain will remember the delight that Amesbury gives them when they enter its pleasant street. Amesbury House is charmingly situated on the river-side, and here Gay, the poet, stayed when it was the residence of the notable Duke of Queensbury. I happened to be there in 1873, and in the week that I was there two birds of a kind supposed to be extinct in England, the bustard, were killed. This may give some idea of how solitary the plain must be, and since writing the above I came across an excellent paragraph concerning Addison's recollections of his youth there, edited by John Morley: 'A man of Addison's imagination could hardly fail to be impressed by the character of the scenery in which his childhood was passed. No one who has travelled on a summer's day across Salisbury Plain, with its vast canopy of sky, and its open tracts of undulating down-land, relieved by no shadows except such as are thrown by a passing cloud, and the great circle of Stonehenge, will forget the delightful sense of refreshment and repose produced by the descent into the valley of the Avon.

The sounds of human life rising from the villages after the long solitude of the plain, the shade of the deep woods, the coolness of the river, like all streams rising in the chalk, clear and peaceful, are equally delicious to the sense and the imagination. It was doubtless the recollection of these scenes that inspired Addison in his paraphrase of the twenty-third Psalm—

> '"The Lord my pasture shall prepare
> And feed me with a Shepherd's care.
>
> . . . .
>
> When in the sultry glebe I faint,
> Or on the thirsty mountain pant,
> To fertile vales and dewy meads
> My weary, wand'ring steps He leads,
> Where peaceful rivers, soft and slow,
> Amid the verdant landscape flow."'

Addison's father became afterwards Dean of Lichfield, which was an excellent appointment; and Addison himself went to Charterhouse, where he acquired the classical knowledge that did him such service in after-time. Charterhouse did not then stand amongst the leading public schools; Rugby also, unlike Eton, Harrow, and Winchester, was little known.

He was especially careful in all words when he wrote, that they should be the very best to express in detail what he meant, and there is a somewhat amusing instance of this which appeared in some recently discovered MSS.: 'A sentence in one of the papers on the *Pleasures of Imagination* shows by the various stages through which it passed before the form became satisfactory to the writer, what nice attention he gave to the balance-rhythm, and lucidity of his periods. In its original shape the sentence was written thus :—

'" For this reason we find the poets always crying up a country life, where nature is left to herself, and appears to the best advantage."

'This is rather bald, and the MS. is accordingly corrected as follows :—

'" For this reason we find all Fancifull men, and ye poets in particular still in love with a country life; where Nature is left to herself and furnishes out all ye variety of scenes y^t are most delightful to ye Imagination."

'The next text as it stands is this :—

'" For this reason we always find the poet in love with a country life, where nature appears in the greatest perfection, and furnishes out all those scenes that are most apt to delight the imagination."'

This is what appears in the *Spectator*, No. 414, and is certainly the best. But Wharton in his essay on Pope even says that Addison was so precise in his wording that he would often stop the press to alter a preposition or conjunction. Addison's knowledge of the Latin language was much more complete and profound, as Macaulay admits, for he had travelled by the means of a government pension in many parts of Europe, including Italy; and in his prime of life the Italian Renaissance was in its height. All the minor Latin poets were familiar to school-boys of talent, and this was the time when Italian mansions crowded out, and destroyed the picturesque gabled halls of the

English landlords; some, indeed, of the latter are left in all counties, but England in Addison's time, if it could be seen, was like the dream of an antiquary.

He left Charterhouse in 1687 at the age of fifteen, and was entered at Queen's College, Oxford. In some two years he left, and a copy of his Latin verses fell into the hands of Dr. Lancaster, who was the Fellow of the college, but afterwards became the Provost, and he thought so highly of them that he managed to secure for him a demyship of Magdalen. Addison became a Probationary Fellow, and in 1698 he was an actual Fellow, an honour he retained for thirteen years. While travelling on the Continent, Addison heard of the death of his father, who had reached the high office of Dean of Lichfield; his own fortunes were at a very low ebb at this time, but within three years he became Under-Secretary of State, and rose from one post to another, until he was enabled to retire with comparative affluence from public life.

Through the influence of the celebrated publisher, Jacob Tonson, aided also by Lord Halifax, Addison became a member of the Kit Cat Club. Halifax was at all times a warm friend of Addison, and when he left his office as High Treasurer, and was succeeded by Godolphin, the latter asked him, as he was a man of letters, to name any one who could write a poem that would worthily celebrate Blenheim. Halifax refused, because he said that he would never recommend any one of parts and learning to celebrate a ministry, 'who had neither the justice nor generosity to make it worth his while;' and on being assured that this was an error, he named Addison. Boyle, the Chancellor of the Exchequer, was sent to interview him, and, according to Pope, he found him in a very humble lodging indeed. The poem is not perhaps very excellent, but one verse, and that the best, may be worth recording, for a great national calamity of which it speaks:—

> 'Twas then great Marlbro's mighty soul was proved,
> That, in the shock of charging hosts unmoved,
> Amidst confusion, horror, and despair,
> Examined all the dreadful scenes of war;
> In peaceful thought the field of death surveyed,
> To fainting squadrons sent the timely aid,
> Inspired repulsed battalions to engage,
> And taught the doubtful battle where to rage.
> So when an angel, by divine command,
> With rising tempests shakes a guilty land,
> Such as of late o'er pale Britannia passed,
> Calm and serene he drives his furious blast,
> And, pleased the Almighty's orders to perform,
> Rides in the whirlwind, and directs the storm.'

There is a line in this that commemorates one of the most fearful hurricanes that ever passed over England. This was the great hurricane of 1703, and in every county there are records of it. Houses were blown down, as were also steeples and barns, and the wrecks and the loss of life were something that caused mourning over half of England at the sea-ports. It is greatly to Addison's credit that he saved enough money from his appointments, and from the sale of the *Spectator* and *Tatler*, to purchase Bilton Hall. The *Spectator*, of course, is not so much read now as it was, but it will always bear perusal, and that with advantage.

Sir Roger de Coverley will live as long as the Vicar of Wakefield, and it certainly is an admirable record of the best class of country gentleman of the seventeenth and eighteenth centuries—a class that has not been quite extinguished in the nineteenth, though the facilities which railways give of journeys to London have much altered their character.

He was, Addison says, a Worcestershire gentleman of ancient family, and his great-grandfather invented the famous dance that bore his name. When Sir Roger went as a young man to London, he often supped with Lord Rochester and Sir George Etheridge, and fought a duel on his first coming to town. At fifty-six he was gay and hearty, and loved the company of mankind. His tenants grew rich under him, and he was a distinguished chairman of the Quarter Sessions, especially versed in the clauses of the game laws. So seldom does Sir Roger change his servants 'that you would take his valet-de-chambre for his brother, his butler is grey-headed, and his coachman has the look of a Privy Councillor.' His chaplain was chosen not for his learning, but for his clear voice, his amiable temper, and his great skill at backgammon; and so far had his choice been a wise one, that for thirty years there had not been a single law-suit in the parish; for if neighbours fell out they placed their differences before him, and in a few rare cases only they appealed to Sir Roger.

He was, Addison says, the 'landlord' of the whole congregation at church, and occupied his family pew with great regularity, allowing no one to sleep except himself; and 'if by chance he has been surprised into a nap during the sermon, upon recovering out of it he stands up and looks about him, and if he sees anybody else nodding, either wakes them himself or sends his servant to them.' On leaving the church he goes down from his square pew in the chancel and all the

congregation rise, not attempting to leave the building until he has departed. This is not an unknown feature near Rugby. There is by Ayston, not far from Uppingham, a fine old church, picturesquely situated among woods, and the rector, Sir J. Henry Fludyer, has till recent times taken an active part in the services of the church. He is also the lord of the manor, and when the service is completed all the congregation rise and stand until he has left the building. Not very far from this is Preston church, which has many singular but

Bilton Ch. Rugby

interesting features, though it has been sadly modernised and the old appearance swept away. Sir Roger's end is most pathetically told, and the utterly brokendown servants and retainers who had known him so long are well described; and, indeed, we cannot but think sometimes that if the Irish landlords of his time had followed more closely in his steps, the country with untold natural beauties might have been happy and wealthy in a very high degree.

Bilton church is charmingly situated among trees and rustic scenes, and its entrance is near to the hall. The tower belongs to fourteenth century architecture, but the spire is of somewhat later construction. The church contains monuments to the Boughton family —a family that figures so conspicuously in this part of the country. The living is a rectory valued in the king's books at £16, 10s. 7½d., but now worth over £600.

'In pursuance of an agreement between the lord of the manor of Bilton and others, about the year 1660, for the enclosure of Bilton, forty-two acres of the common were set out for the use of the poor of the said town for ever. The whole is now cultivated; about eight acres are let as garden ground. There are sixteen or seventeen houses on the poor's land paying with their gardens £1 a year each, 1833,' but these terms are advanced. In the year 1783 Langton Freeman, by will, directed his executors to lay out £400 in establishing a charity school in this parish; the master receives £20 yearly from the estate.

Bilton Grange is situated about a mile from Bilton Hall, and there are no less than three roads to it, all of nearly equal length. There was an old house, of which part remains, but the new part is a fine brick mansion, which was commenced in 1846 from designs of Augustus

Welby Pugin, the most excellent architect of Gothic in his day, and indeed he has had few equals since. It occupied three years in building, and was a happy illustration of the style of the time of Henry VII., when the Tudor or Perpendicular architecture, as it is equally termed, was at its best. Oak panels and oak floors ap-

Entering Dunchurch.

pear in its interior which is quite worthy of the exterior. It has been sold to the Rev. W. Earle, and converted into a large preparatory school. Wm. Lancaster was the next previous owner.

Close to Bilton Grange is Dunchurch, a very well-built country village that gives the name to a rural deanery. The church is dedicated to St. Peter, and is in very good preservation, and belongs to the latter part of the fourteenth century. In the reign of Stephen, Dunchurch belonged to Clement, and he gave all his lands to the monks of Pipewell.

Pipewell Abbey was in Northampton, but within a moderate distance from Rugby, and it had a very signal history. It was a Cistercian house, and founded by William Butevileyn. Here Richard I. in the first year of his reign held a great council. It was attended by nearly all the bishops of England and Ireland, besides abbots and priors, and many laymen of great influence. Green, in his history of Richard, after speaking of his love of adventure, his pride in his personal strength, and other parallel characteristics, says that 'he was at heart a statesman, cool and patient in the execution of his plans as he was bold in their conception.' The vacant bishoprics were filled, and he raised money for his memorable crusade. I was not able to find any traces of the abbey, though in some Warwickshire histories it is said that the remains, though very slight, still exist. This abbey was wealthy, as at the dissolution its revenues were recorded at £283 per annum. Pipewell, it is said, stood in Rockingham Forest, so that the state business might be enlightened by the royal chase. This forest was one of the largest in the kingdom, and lay from Northampton to Stamford, or about thirty-three miles, and its average breadth was about eight miles. Until very recent years wild deer were occasionally met with in it. Twice was Dunchurch confiscated to the Crown, and in the reign of Mary it was purchased by Sir Thomas Leigh, and afterwards it descended to Lord Dunsmore. There is in the church a very singular monument to Thomas Newcombe, which is almost unique. He was the king's printer in the

Dunchurch Parish Church

time of Charles II., James II., and William III. He founded an almshouse, which was rebuilt in 1818 by subscription. His monument is preserved by folding doors of white marble, which are still in perfect condition.

A notable feature in Dunchurch is the stocks. These may yet be seen in many country villages, and they were even in use in comparatively late times. In Henry IV.'s time an Act was passed, A.D. 1405, that every village and every town in England should be provided with stocks, and this was done. James I., in 1606, passed an Act that all persons convicted of drunkenness should be fined five shillings and placed

Stocks, Dunchurch

for six hours in the stocks. These stocks were never intended for cases of felony, but misdemeanour; and the great idea was that a prisoner so exposed should be a warning to his fellows. In 1623 James I. for some cause brought in a supplementary Act confirming what he had done before. Not only was the captive a public object, but the achings of the stocks, as we have learned from a very high authority, were dreadful. This authority is no less than the Lord Chancellor Eldon, the year before he was raised to the Chancellorship. He was staying at Lord Dacre's seat, Hoo Park, in Hertfordshire, and on a summer afternoon he was walking in a neighbouring village with a country magistrate who was also on a visit to Lord Dacre. Speaking of the stocks and the pillory, he said that he had often sent men to the stocks, and he had often seen men in, and he wondered whether they were so very unpleasant as some people averred. He thought not. When his friend said that he had a key in his pocket and asked him if he would like to try what the effect of the stocks was, and he said, after seeing that the lanes were clear, that he thought he would for a short time. Now his friend unfortunately was of an absent mind, and he had scarcely left the Chief Justice of the Court of Common Pleas when his thoughts reverted to some other subject in which he was deeply interested, and he wandered up to Hoo Park. Great was the shock when he was asked where he had left his friend, and the fleetest servant was despatched with the key to release the Chief Justice, who returned to Hoo not, it is said, in the best of humours; for while he was in durance, the tale goes that some market carts slowly rambled back from the market, and much regret was expressed to see any one so well habited in such a place. In great anger he called out to them that he was the Chief Justice of Common Pleas, and some of them must at once get him free, even if they broke the stocks; but what was his horror when he heard them say that it was shocking to see so very well-dressed a man in such a state!

It is said that the tale was kept quiet until there happened to be a trial for some illegal committal to the stocks, and the sufferer brought an action against the bench of justices. For the defence the counsel, who was a 'serjeant,' claimed only farthing damages, as

In Dunchurch.

the stocks were merely a slight and not always an unpleasant refuge, the prisoner being surrounded often by friends, and sitting in warm sunshine, etc., etc., till the judge interrupted him with, 'Brother, were you ever in the stocks?' 'Certainly not,' was the astonished reply. 'Ah, well, I thought as much,' the judge said, 'I have been.'

We return now to the western side of **Rugby**, and pass again into Warwickshire, and there are several roads to Stoneleigh besides those that have been alluded to. The train will take us to Birdingbury, a small village on the river Leam, which is spanned by a fine bridge built in 1873, as the old one had been destroyed by the floods of that year.

KENILWORTH

From Stoneleigh to Kenilworth the road is simply delightful, and this part of the country is among the most rustic in England. The Avon winds through pleasant meadow lands, and is a real English river. The Rhine I know well, and nobody would compare its grand beauty with the Avon; but as it often occurred to me when you leave any well-known continental resort of beauty you find little behind. The French villages are not picturesque, and, with some exceptions and those not many, the same may be said of the German ones. The wars and wars that desolated Europe were not, it is true, destructive of the grand ecclesiastical buildings that were guarded by the episcopacy, who were supreme, for the quarrels were between different nationalities that cared little for the homesteads of the people. But in England there were no invaders, and the wars were civil. Indeed, it is well worthy of note that in the Wars of the Roses the trade of England was little disturbed, and the judges went their circuits in quiet. The castles and the surroundings of the great residences of the nobles had innumerable retainers, who were without occupation, and lived on their rent-rolls.

Probably the bulk of these were descendants from their ancestors, and they went on multiplying until, as in the

Wars of the Roses, the result of the great congregations was a contest to thin them out. In *As you like It* there is a very suggestive line that is perhaps overlooked sometimes. When Rosalind and Celia were in Ardennes Forest and wondering where they could purchase some food, Corin the shepherd appears, and Touchstone the jester calls out to him pompously, ' Hollo, you clown ! ' and Rosalind suddenly checks him with, ' Peace, fool ; he is not thy kinsman.' Indeed, in old times, when the feudal system was at its height, the kinsmen of the nobles were often troublesome hangers-on, and this might throw some little light upon the records of Kenilworth.

Happily, there is a spa at Leamington that is very near Kenilworth, which is said to be of great value in many internal disorders, and this brings a vast number of visitors, so that Kenilworth Castle is not as so many other places of interest are, buried in obscurity.

Perhaps in *Kenilworth* Sir Walter Scott went rather too far in bringing in Amy Robsart. No doubt the scenes are most dramatic, and, indeed, almost the essence of the work, but, as a matter of fact, the Countess of Leicester met her end some two or three years before the grand festivities at Kenilworth, which, so far as we know or can judge, have no parallel for lavish costliness in our history. But at the same time there is hardly a doubt that Scott's careful examination of the old castle has been the result of a painstaking search, and his description is well worth recording. Sir Walter Scott says that the Earl of Leicester spent £60,000 in improving the castle, which he considers would be equal to fully half a million now, but nothing is more illusive than the ordinary comparisons of the value of money between this time and that. In some things we are much cheaper, as, for example, a journey from Liverpool could be done now for as many shillings as it would have cost pounds; but in a case like building a castle, where

Kenilworth Castle Porter's Lodge.

the labour and materials were so much at Leicester's disposal, it is probable that the sum named would more nearly represent a million of money of our day.

'The outer wall,' Scott says, 'of this splendid and gigantic structure enclosed seven acres, a part of which was occupied by extensive stables, and by a pleasure garden, with its trim arbours and parterres, and the rest formed the large base-court or outer yard of the noble Castle. The lordly structure itself, which rose near the centre of this spacious enclosure, was composed of a huge pile of magnificent castellated buildings, apparently of different ages, surrounding an inner court, and bearing in the names attached to each portion of the magnificent mass, and in the armorial bearings which were there

Kenilworth Castle.

blazoned, the emblems of mighty chiefs who had long passed away, and whose history, could ambition have lent ear to it, might have read a lesson to the haughty favourite, who had now acquired and was augmenting the fair domain. A large and massive Keep, which formed the citadel of the Castle, was of uncertain though great antiquity. It bore the name of Cæsar, perhaps from its resemblance to that in the Tower of London so called. Some antiquaries ascribe its foundation to the time of Kenelph, from whom the Castle had its name, a Saxon king of Mercia.' Since Scott wrote *Kenilworth*, the belief in this origin to its name has certainly increased. In Elizabeth's day it was called Killingworth, but now it is attributed to the words Kenelph and 'worth,' the Saxon for a dwelling-place or house.

'Old John of Gaunt, "time-honoured Lancaster," had widely extended the Castle, erecting that noble and massive pile which yet bears the name of Lancaster's Buildings; and Leicester himself had outdone the former possessors, princely and powerful as they were, by erecting another immense structure, which now lies crushed under its own ruins, the monument of its owner's ambition. The external wall of this royal Castle was, on the south and west sides, adorned and defended by a lake partly artificial, across which Leicester had constructed a stately bridge, that Elizabeth might enter the Castle by a path hitherto untrodden, instead of the usual entrance to the northward, over which he had erected a gate-house, or barbican, which still exists, and is equal in extent, and superior in architecture, to the baronial castle of many a northern chief.

'Beyond the lake lay an extensive chase, full of red deer, fallow deer, roes, and every species of game, and abounding with lofty trees, from amongst which the extended front and massive towers of the Castle were seen to rise in majesty and beauty. . . . The bed of the lake is but a rushy swamp; and the massive ruins of the Castle only serve to show what their splendour once was, and to impress on the musing visitor the transitory value of human possessions.'

The gate-house, which is passed on the public road, is a fine massive building with four octagonal towers at the corners, and the masonry is of very fine quality indeed. There are two shapely gables which were added in the seventeenth century, and only the angle of one appears in the sketch, but probably the view from the other side where they are seen is finer, and they, indeed, compare well with the older parts, and the gate-house is quite a roomy abode. It was converted into a residence during the Parliamentary War, and was occupied by one Hawkesworth who was a Parliamentary officer, and to him was intrusted the demolition of the castle. Sad indeed as the havoc was, which the Parliamentary party inflicted on the churches and wayside crosses, which included even the Eleanor Crosses, the demolition of the great baronial houses that Charles brought about—for it was impossible that Cromwell could allow such strongholds to remain for a menace—was even quite as regrettable.

But the record of Scott, though from its dramatic picturesqueness it brings Kenilworth more prominently before us than any other, is in import not to be compared with its former history. Kenilworth was rebuilt by Geoffrey de Clinton, who was Lord Chamberlain and Treasurer to Henry I., but it passed afterwards to the Crown. He seems, though starting from a somewhat obscure position, to have been a man of great ability, and even had a judgeship, but the most important of all its records is its possession by Simon de Montfort.

Pope Innocent III. had been the most exacting and oppressive of Pontiffs, and his successor, Honorius, was much more at variance with the English ecclesiastics than is commonly supposed. When the Archbishop of York was excommunicated, which, indeed, was rather a high-handed measure, the people flocked round him all the more, and defied the papal power over their own country. Even such men as Grossteste, the most excellent of prelates, concurred, and the papacy had sunk much by the removal to Avignon, in a charming valley on the left side of the Rhone, where the popes were the nominees of the Kings of France, during, indeed, the Edwardian period. Simon de Montfort was an English patriot, but he was of foreign extraction, and he was devoted to the popular cause, though related by marriage to the king. Kenilworth was the seat of the de Montforts, and there are doubtless some of their relics in architecture still remaining there; and Simon de Montfort, senior, had taken up arms against the king in the popular cause, although for Edward I. he had a great admiration.

On the 4th of August, 1265, Edward appeared on the heights above Evesham. He had been for a time in the custody of Simon de Montfort, the elder, and with his soldierly skill he strongly desired to avenge old days. It was at the battle of Lewes that de Montfort defeated Edward and his father, Henry, and made them both prisoners. This battle was a very remarkable affair, and it would be impossible to go into half the causes of the quarrels between the king and the barons; but Simon de Montfort was victorious, and the King Henry and his son Edward were both taken prisoners and strongly guarded. In the course of some short time the prince escaped from his confinement, and the battle of Evesham was the result. There was a very dramatic part in this that connects Kenilworth with the day. Kenilworth had been the stronghold of the barons in their struggle with the king, and after the escape of Edward, Leicester required the king to proclaim him a traitor, which he did; but Simon de Montfort, the elder, sent to his son to join him at the forthcoming battle of Evesham. Prince Edward met the younger Simon de Montfort by Kenilworth and utterly routed him and took his banners away. When Simon de Montfort was in battle array at Evesham he saw the banners that had been taken at Kenilworth, and supposed they indicated the arrival of his son. But when he saw Edward's army, he said: 'Now, God have mercy on our souls, for our bodies are Prince Edward's.' He and his son Henry were slain in the battle; and so the wars of the barons were ended for the time at least.

One of the next features we read of in the history of Kenilworth is its occupation by John of Gaunt, 'time-honoured Lancaster.' Gaunt made extensive additions to Kenilworth, and some of them remain, though in ruins, but they are very beautiful architecturally. This was only one of the great residences of

Lancaster. He owned Hertford Castle, and was the Lord of the Manor. This castle was built at least a century before the Conquest, but hardly any trace of it remains, and the present castle was built in the time of Charles I. He also owned the magnificent Savoy Palace on the Thames, of which we have fortunately some few illustrations left. This, had it survived like the tower, would probably now be the happy hunting-ground for all architects who could have entered its close. Part of it was standing so lately as 1711, and perhaps even later still. But some drawings are preserved of this, and, unlike the castles of the period, which were frowning strongholds externally, the walls of London protected it, and the builders could devote themselves to architectural beauty. And this, if we will only look at the churches and dwellings of the period, would show that even builders and masons were born with a sense of architectural beauty. I have seen a contract for a church in Cheshire that is very excellent as an example of architecture, and there were no plans as there would be now. The builder was directed to have so many bays with windows of so many lights, and everything was to be in fair form. This dated at the time of Richard III. Even the farm-houses and porches, and everything that was built, was of such pleasing form in early days that builders might have said with Ovid:

'Et quod tentabam scribere versus erat.'

John II. of France was captured at Poitiers, though he really showed something like a commander's ability, but the battle was actually lost by the French, who numbered nearly five to one, and who were in their own country. By an attack on the rear, where the Dauphin was, and the danger of any member of the royal house falling into the hands of an enemy at once, caused the knights and officers to flee with him; and the Duke of Orleans, who commanded another division, seeing the confusion, fancied all was lost, and fled too. King John was taken prisoner, and was under the charge of John of Gaunt. It is not improbable that part of his captivity was spent at Kenilworth, where John of Gaunt was living in great splendour. But much time was passed at his residence, Savoy Palace, and he received nothing but kind hospitable treatment, though he never could forget that he was a captive, and said to those even who wished him well, 'How can I sing the Lord's song in a strange land?'

John of Gaunt lived, of course, in the days of Edward II., one of the most feeble and useless of monarchs, indeed it has often been a matter of wonder to me how such an outcast could have had such a noble father and such a noble son. In another way John of Gaunt was connected with the surroundings of Rugby, for he was a close adherent and friend of Wycliffe, who held the living of Lutterworth in Leicestershire, and whose name is a text-book even now. Lutterworth Church has undergone many alterations and modernisings since Wycliffe was there, but much of the old building remains. A pulpit is shown where he preached. It is of black oak, and, though the style would suggest a somewhat later period, there is no reason to suppose that at any rate part of it (for it has been altered) may not have been contemporaneous with the great Lollard. Their dwellings were not far distant, and a close alliance was formed between the Lord of Kenilworth and the incumbent of Lutterworth. 'The attack of Wycliffe began precisely at the moment when the church of the Middle Ages had sunk to its lowest point of spiritual decay. The transfer of the Papacy to Avignon robbed it of much of the awe in which it had been held, for not only had the Popes sunk into creatures of the French kings, but their greed and extortion produced almost universal revolt. The assumption of a right to dispose of all ecclesiastical benefices in ecclesiastical patronage, the imposition of direct taxes on the clergy, the intrusion of foreign priests into English livings and English sees produced a fierce hatred and contempt of Rome which never slept till the Reformation. The people scorned a "French Pope" and threatened his legates with stoning when they arrived. The wit of Chaucer flouted the wallet of "pardons hot from Rome," and Piers the ploughman and Wat Tyler were in strong sympathy with the people, but not with John of Gaunt; and the reason was simply this that though he was at one with them all in their antagonism to the Roman Church as far as her rule of England was concerned, John of Gaunt was a leader of the barons, and though indeed they stood up at first fairly against undue kingly influence, it was quite clear that they would lord it just as much themselves over the people when they had put down the prerogatives of the Crown and the Church. Worthless as John of Gaunt seems to us, it was with him that Wycliffe allied himself in the first effort he made for the reform of the Church. As yet his quarrel was not with its doctrine but with its practice. It was on the principles of Ockham that he defended the parliament's indignant refusal of the "tribute" which was claimed by the papacy, the expulsion of bishops from office by the Duke of Lancaster, and the taxation of Church lands. But his treatise on "the Kingdom of God" (*de dominio divino*) shows how different his aims were really from the selfish aims of the men with whom he acted.'

Wycliffe was working hard with John of Gaunt, and doing all he could to advance ecclesiastical reform, when the insurrection of the peasants under Wat Tyler broke out, and this quite crippled all the work he had done. The Lancastrian party was annihilated, and the dispute between the baronage and the Church was for the time ended by a common danger. The friars took advantage of the outbreak by taxing Wycliffe with being the chief cause, and they said he was a sower of strife who, by his serpent-like instigation, had set the serf against his lord; and, though Wycliffe treated such words with disdain, some of his followers were not quite so free from blame as he was. But, even if the peasant revolt had not deprived him of much support, his doctrines were sadly against his advancement, for he had begun to protest against what are termed the cardinal beliefs of the Church. The doctrine of transubstantiation was the stronghold of the Mediæval Church, for it was held that the performance of this miracle by even a lowly priest placed its performer above all princes, and in the year 1381 Wycliffe issued a formal denial of transubstantiation. This, of course, led to the great antagonism between the Lollards and the ecclesiastical authorities, and commenced a severance between the English people and Rome that only ended in Thomas Cromwell's time when monasteries were put down. Oxford declared strongly for Wycliffe, but was put down by the Archbishop Courtenay, and nothing can show more strongly the great power of Wycliffe than the fears of Courtenay to proceed against him when he was summoned to appear before the Council, and absolutely refused, and even petitioned the king that he might be allowed to prove the doctrine he had asserted. He went so far as to say that tithes should go to the maintenance of the poor, and the clergy be supported by the free offerings of their congregations, and that excommunication from Rome should not prevent any man from being engaged in any civil employment or make him liable as it did to imprisonment and confiscation. He was summoned to the convocation at Oxford, and quite perplexed his opponents with his scholastic knowledge and argumentative powers, and the result of all was his expulsion from the University and his retirement to Lutterworth. He was summoned to appear at Rome, but said that his failing health would not permit him to do so, and in a characteristic reply he told the Pope that when Christ was on earth

He was the poorest and humblest of men and cast away all worldly authority, and he recommended the Pope 'as a counsel of his own' to do the same. The energy of his reply, as has been stated, was almost a mark that he knew his end was near, and soon after, while hearing mass in Lutterworth church, he was struck with paralysis and died the next day. The chair is still shown in which he died in the year 1384. There is a narrow river called the Swift that runs by Lutterworth and enters

Lutterworth Church

the Avon by Brownsover not far from Rugby station after passing by Cotesbach and Churchover, and forty years after his death his remains were exhumed and cast into the Swift near the churchyard in a spot which is still pointed out.

Here we are quite within one of the most Roman parts of England. We have York and Chester that are, it may be, more notably connected with history, but the quiet life of the Roman settlers was always away from fortified cities, and the finest villas are found in country parts; and it has often been thought that the Romans left in country parts records and relics behind them that are even now developing. Dr. Temple in a fine essay speaks of ancient Rome as a centre where the people had all the wisdom of age with the energy of youth, and that makes their history so intensely interesting to us. But it has often been thought that there was a Roman element left in England that is still developing. We know that when Honorius left for Rome he left behind him great multitudes of his country-men and country-women, who had settled in England for life, and it may be that our skies were fitted to retain the Roman type while it vanished under those of Italy and all other Roman settlements. One thing is certain, that if we look at any old statues or busts, such as Marcus Aurelius, Julius Cæsar, or Vespasian, or indeed any other, we shall see the most pronounced English faces, and, as has been remarked, if we visit any ancient collection of statues in Italy we shall almost think we are among our countrymen, and those who are outside are like foreigners.

It was a century after Cæsar's attack upon Britain that Claudius conquered the island, and he did his work thoroughly. In about thirty years he and his generals had completely subdued the country, and there does not seem to have been so much ruin and pillage as in some other Roman conquests. Indeed, no colony appears to have adapted itself more thoroughly to Roman ways than Britain. The natives worked the mines and helped to build the great roads that even yet are among the important highways of England. Watling Street was the most important, and extended from Kent to Cardigan Bay, and also the Firth of Forth. For a considerable distance it forms the boundary between Leicestershire and Warwickshire, and enters Staffordshire at Fazeley, a short way to the south of Tamworth. It then runs in a very direct line through Staffordshire, and enters Shropshire by Sheriff-Hales, and then it runs by Wallington on to Shrewsbury, and from thence it proceeded on its way to the north. There are old remains of villas and towns along the road, and many more lie buried under the soil, perhaps only a short distance below. Just before entering Shrewsbury the road passes by Wroxeter, or the ancient Uriconium. Now the remains of this interesting place show that it must have been an important city, and well in accord with natives of Britain. Some of the relics in precious metals show also that it was the seat of people of wealth and refinement, and there is no doubt that a not very expensive excavation would reveal many details of Roman occupation, and many treasures. Three Roman roads, however, would seem to have crossed the country—Watling Street, Ickneld Street, and the Via Devana which led to Chester. There were also the Roman towns of Etocetum and Pennocrucium upon the road, and though this may perhaps have been rather a favourite district with the Romans, we find some even more beautiful remains of Roman villas in Gloucestershire and Oxford, and in many parts of the counties that lie to the south of the Thames, and, indeed, it is often sad to see how these have been broken up most ruthlessly by either Picts, or Scots, or intruders of whom we know so little. Ermine Street ran from London to Lincoln, and though it is continued past that city, its traces are lost. This was only a system of the roads that the Romans built in England. Watling Street went from Richborough to Anglesea, and there are traces of it even in the sea. The Fosse was the highway between Bath and Lincoln, and Ickneld Street or Icneld Street went from Norwich to the capital city. The four Roman roads traversed at least 1250 miles, and they were engineered under every possible disadvantage, for the stone had often to be brought from great distances, and the makers were compelled to employ the unskilled labour of the native Britons, though, indeed, we may well suppose that the engineers attached to their legions kept the inhabitants in the right way. The present Roman road through Rutland does not, indeed, exactly adhere to the lines of Ermine Street, but it so nearly coincides that we may take the present road for the original street. If the suggestion of Mr. Laird, that the name Ermine Street is derived from the Saxon word 'Herman,' a warrior, is just, this would account for much; because the Roman commanders, who certainly laid out the lines of all the roads, and superintended their construction, would be looked upon by subsequent dwellers as the conquerors. It certainly is more reasonable than the fanciful definitions and derivations that have been tacked upon it. Selden traces its name to 'Irmensul,' a name given by the Saxons to Mercury, who, according to some interpretations of Roman mythology, presided over highways in some perfunctory manner. And some other authorities have agreed in deriving the name from 'Armyinth,' a British word, because it crosses mountains and pathless places, and indeed, if we followed such shadowy logic, almost anything might be made out of anything. There are plenty of traces of this grand road, and Roman remains have been found. Some parts of its ancient construction about Casterton and Tickencote are well worthy of study. The Roman roads differed entirely from ours in their construction, and in almost every particular. The highways of Macadam which traverse our counties were suggested to that almost untaught genius by the following considerations: He found that if cinders and shale and stone-clippings were thrown over any road across a piece of marsh land, they gradually formed a hard bed, if only this bed were kept dry, so that, without a solid foundation like the Romans built all through England, a lasting road could be formed.

There are along the Roman roads many ancient towns that were built in the Danish and Saxon times, and some few places may be mentioned, in conclusion, that are within reach of the great highway. The Roman Fosse crosses the river Avon at Bretford, which is a joint hamlet with Brandon. It is a small village, and is interesting as having been once held by the celebrated Geoffrey de Clinton, whose son in the time of Henry II. founded a cell for black nuns there. The joint hamlet of Brandon is of great beauty, and the illustration shows one of our most beautiful country villages. There are good residences in it and round it, and it does almost seem as if it were the model home,

where any one would willingly end 'life's fitful fever.' Almost joining Brandon is the charming village of Wolston. It is approached by a long bridge across the Avon, and is exceedingly picturesque. Rods and lines are generally seen over the bridge, and the Avon is a halting-place there for perch, and roach, and dace, but they say that trout have for long ceased to make it their rendezvous. The church is very interesting, and has a valuable amount of Norman work; though there are later examples of architecture in it, some of which date from the years of the dissolution of monasteries. There was an alien priory here, of which some part still remains.

The view of the church from the south-east, which is here given, shows a regular cruciform structure, and the chancel window belongs to the fourteenth century. In the reign of Henry I. the manor and

Wolston.

lordship of Wolston belonged to Roger de Fredvill, and he generously divided his lands among the monks of Burton and Kenilworth, Alcester and Coombe. The manor soon after came into possession of the Turvilles. Sir Richard Bagot afterwards, in the time of Richard II., possessed it, and his daughters afterwards passed it over to the canons of Kenilworth, but without a licence;

and then it was seized by the king, Henry VI., from whom it came among others to the members of the Throckmorton family, a name that so often appears in Cowper's letters.

From Wolston and Brinklow the Roman Fosse proceeds to Leicestershire, and enters that county by the High Cross, near Wibtoft and Copston. This latter was given by Geoffrey de Wrice in the twelfth

Wolston Church, Rugby.

year of William I. (1077-78) to the monastery of St. Nicholas at Angers, and after the dissolution of monasteries it was granted to Charles Brandon, Duke of Suffolk, from whose family it afterwards came by purchase to Basil, Lord Feilding, who was afterwards the Earl of Denbigh.

Claybrooke is a large parish that comprehends an

area of some four miles in length, by nearly two and a half in breadth, and is estimated to contain 4000 acres of land. The parish is divided into two villages, which are named in various ways. The church stands in Upper Claybrooke, and is on the great highway that separates Lutterworth from Hinckley. There is in Claybrooke Lane a piece of quickset hedge that betokens

one side of the Fosse. The church, which may be approached from the high road between Hinckley and Lutterworth, or else there is a much more pleasant route across the fields from Rugby, is a fine example of the best fourteenth century style, but its inside has been obliterated by what is called restoration, and flimsy chairs take the place of the fine old oak pews, and this is only another weary example of the demolition of the fine old parish churches of England. The distance to High Cross is not considerable, and at a short distance to the west side is a tumulus called Cloudsley Bush, about which Dugdale offers some suggestions and conjectures, but nothing really explanatory has come to light. From this high elevation, it is said, and perhaps, indeed, truly said, that with the aid of a spy-glass no

At Ullethorpe.

less than fifty-seven churches can be seen. Macaulay wrote a history of Claybrooke at the beginning of this century, and he gives a just account of how we have neglected to see the old roysterings in their right form. The wakes at Claybrooke were met by farmers and cottagers with great hilarity, and these were almost a scene of dissipation at times, but the worst of all was the attendance from the Leicester towns, where working was carried on, and even in the villages, for there was always a week of idleness and dissipation. Claybrooke is situated between one and two miles from Ullesthorpe station, and the country all round it is of great interest. Great was my surprise to see a bittern, a bird of great scarcity for a number of years, rise up from a pond, and fortunately there was no double-barrelled gun

At Ullesthorpe.

about to end its days 'after its life of hazard.' The rustic scenes that are here shown will give a fair idea of the character of the country.

The Rambles round Rugby have embraced a wider area than was at first proposed, but then the places are so accessible by railways that it must be held as an excuse.

If, for example, though without going very far from Rugby, a trip should be taken to the neighbourhood of Coombe Abbey, or the beautiful neighbourhood that lies between that and Coventry, the distance would be easily met by the choice of two lines to return by; there is Shilton or Bulkington on the London and North-Western line, and Brandon and Wolston on a branch of the same that lies towards the south, and this also applies to the routes in Northampton and Leicestershire. So that it may be fairly said a long walk will generally bring a pedestrian within reach of two lines, and if one does not suit his time there is a chance that the other may. The country round Rugby is exceedingly healthy, raised high above the sea, and having an extensive water-shed; it stands very high indeed among the healthful parts of our island. The climate of Warwickshire is mild, and the winds that generally prevail are from the south-west, and this brings a fair amount of rain. Towards the middle of May there are often easterly winds, but the climate does not, as a rule, suffer much from the effects of wet or cold weather. Barley would seem to be the grain which is most commonly grown; but there are good crops of wheat, and many other crops of value. Where the country approaches Leicestershire the permanent grazing lands are more extensive, and in this county we may see the hills pleasantly dotted over with the celebrated cattle and sheep for which it is so famous everywhere. Watling Street, for nearly thirty miles, forms the boundary between Leicester and Warwick, and the three counties join near Dunsland, which lies a short distance to the east of Rugby.

Fuller in his *Worthies* says : ' It bordereth on more counties than any other in England, being more in number. It is as fruitful and populous as any in England, insomuch that sixteen several towns with their churches, have at one view been discovered therein by my eyes (other men have discovered two-and-thirty), which I confess none of the best ; and God grant that those who are sharper-sighted may hereafter never see fewer. Sure I am that there is as little waste ground in this as in any county in England, no mosses, mears, fells, heaths, which elsewhere fill so many shires with emptiness.'

Fuller's description of Northampton is even truer now than it was when he wrote it. There are in the county something like 630,000 statute acres, and nearly 600,000 are arable and pasture. Fuller is quite correct in saying that Northampton touches nine counties, and this exceeds any other English record, though Cambridge joins eight. The Oolite sandstone that occupies so large a space in this district is very interesting, as it contains the most interesting and remarkable of all fossil relics. But in every direction the country round Rugby is full of interest and beauty, and indeed one or two works might be written in addition to this, that would show up new scenes and landscapes of beauty, with ever so many records of interest. Perhaps, indeed, it would hardly be an exaggeration if we said that for any persons who desired to see England as it was, and greatly such a party is increasing, more even in America than here, for even travelling carriages are now sometimes sent over to England to see the land. If a centre was desired for the Midland Counties, Rugby would stand very high indeed.

INDEX.

Abbey commissioners for dissolution, 147.
Abbey rent-rolls, 130.
Addison, 221-227, 229.
Allingham, Sir Richard Giles, 86.
Amy Robsart, 112, 241.
Anthony Foster, 112.
Architectural styles (Rickman), 124.
Ashby St. Leger, 38, 42, 56.
Ashby de la Zouche, 85.
Ashby de la Zouche canal, 140.
Avon River, 1, 95, 119, 120, 132, 137, 138, 154, 258.

Baginton, 133.
Barnack stone, 212.
Bilton, 221.
,, Hall, 222.
,, Church, 231.
,, Grange, 230.
Blisworth Station, 32.
Blue Boar Inn, Leicester, 66.
Bolingbroke, 95, 97.
Bordesley Abbey, 119.
Bosworth, Battle of, 65, 67.
Boughton, Sir Theodosius poisoned, 138.
Brackenbury, Sir Robert, 69.
Braunston Cleves, 64.
Brinklow, 140, 141.
,, to Rugby, 142.
Britain, Conquest of, by the Romans, 254.

Brownsover, 12, 13.
Bullet Hill, 76.
Burleigh Park, 205.

Caldicott family, 188.
Canock, Staffordshire, 117, 118.
Catesby, 40, 46, 47.
,, Lady, 46.
Catherine of Arragon, 43.
Cavaliers, their Tyranny, 166.
Cave family, 157.
Cedar of Lebanon at Ashby St. Legers, 56.
Coombe Abbey, 89, 142-146.
,, dissolution (Dugdale), 146.
Coventry, 89.
,, Cross, 98.
,, Spires, 95, 134.
,, St Mary's Hall, 92, 99.
,, St. Michael's Church, 92, 100.
,, Holy Trinity, 102.
,, Parliaments at, 104.
,, ,, Indoctorum, 104.
,, ,, Diabolicum, 105.
,, Walls wrecked by Charles after restoration, 91, 92.
Crick, 38, 61, 63.
Cubbington, 114.
Cumnor Church, 112.

Dassett Hills, 77.
Digby, Sir Everard, 48, 59.
,, Kenelm, 48.

unchurch, 233.
,,   Church, 235.
,,   Stocks, 236.
Dunsmore Heath, 4.

EDGEHILL, Battle of, 72, 74, 79, 80.
Edgecott House, 75.
Elizabethan Architecture, 211.
Elizabeth, Princess, Lord Harrington's maid, 144.
Elizabeth's letter to the Bishop of Ely, 218.
Ellesmere, Lord Chancellor, 117.
Erasmus, 131.

FLORE'S HOUSE, 202, 203.
Fosse way (Roman), 1, 257, 260.
Fotheringhay Castle, 100.
Fuller's description of Northampton, 265.

GAUNT, JOHN of, 247.
Gloucester Cathedral, 106.
Gosford Green, Meeting of Bolingbroke and Mowbray at, 94; the combatants banished by Richard II., 98.
Great Bowden, 175.
Green on Edgehill, 79.
Greathead, Samuel, 121.
Greek Architecture, 126, 127.
Grey Friars' Hospital, 103.
Grossteste, Bishop, 193.
Gunpowder Plot: Collapse, Capture, and Execution of conspirators, 52-56.
Guy Fawkes, 46, 48.
Guy's Well and Cliff, 120.

HEAD-MASTER'S HOUSE, Rugby, 26.
Hoggins, father of Countess Burleigh, 209.
Hoggins, Tennyson's Poem, 210.

Holdenby (Holmby), 164, 168-172.
Hood, Vicount, 134.
Hoxton, 49.

IRONSIDES, 82.

KENILWORTH, 114, 240-245, 247.
Keyes of Lambeth, 47.
Kilsby, 38.
Kineton, 75.
'King Charles Tower,' Chester, 81.
Kirby, Old Hall, 173.
Knevett, Sir Thomas, 51.

LANGDALE, SIR MARMADUKE, 84, 85.
Lawrence, Sheriff, 15.
Leamington, 241.
Leicestershire, Agriculture in, 152.
,,   Cattle and Sheep, 152, 264.
,,   Geology, 150.
,,   Roads, 150.
Leicester's Hospital, Warwick, 108.
Leigh, Sir Thomas, 46.
Leigh Family, 116.
Lindsey, Lord, 77.
Lollards, 252.
Lubbenham, 164.
Lutterworth Church, 249.
Lyddington, 193.
Lyddington Manor, 195.

MANTON CHURCH, 196.
,,   Mill, 198.
Market Harboro', 148, 175.
,,   Roman remains, 178.
,,   School, 177.
,,   Church to Dionysius the Areopagite, 179.
Marston Trussel Church, 87.
Maurice, Prince, 84.
Mickle's Ballad of Amy Robsart, 113.

Minster Lovell, 40.
Monteagle, 49.
Montrose, Marquis of, 81.
More, Sir Thomas, 45.

NASEBY CHURCH, 85.
Naseby Woolleys, 86.
New Bilton, 7.
Newbold-on-Avon, 137.
Newnham Regis, 138.
North Kilworth, 158.
Northampton, Earl of, 84.
Nottingham, Charles I. Standard at, 73.

OAKHAM, 198, 199.
,, Hospital of St. John, 205.
Oakley Hall, 181.
Old Quadrangle, Rugby, 28.
Oneley Charity, 138.
Oxford Canal, 140.

PERCY, 46.
Piers Gaveston, 184.
Pipewell Abbey, 22, 178, 234.
Plantagenet, rise of House, 71.
Post and Petrel, or black and white work, 111.
Preston Church, 230.

RADWAY, 75, 76.
Ratcliffes, the, 40.
Richard III., 65, 66.
Rockingham, 180, 182.
,, Castle, 183, 184.
,, Church, 187.
Roman remains, 255-257.
Rupert, Prince, 74, 82.
Rugby Church, 6.
,, Chapel, 37.
,, Masters, 16, 20, 25.
,, School, 9.
,, Village, 10.

SENHOUSE, family of, 53-60.
,, Humphrey, founder of Maryport, 59.
Shelly, R. 45.
Siddons, Mrs., portrait of, 122.
Simon de Montfort, 247.
South Kilworth, 158.
Snelstone Ruins, 194.
Spencer of Althorpe, 74.
Spon Tower Magazine, 134.
Stamford, 206.
,, Bridge, 207.
,, Churches, 208.
Stanford Church, 155.
,, Hall, 158.
Stanley at Bosworth, 68.
Stivichall, oak trees and history, 135, 136.
Stoneleigh Abbey, 114, 116.
,, Abbots, 123.
,, Church, 132.
,, Foundation of, 119.
,, Mausoleum, 132.
,, Village, 132.

TEMPLE, Dr., 34.
Tichbourne, 45.
Theddingworth, 162, 163.
Thorpe, Sir John, 219.
Tresham, 49.
Tripontium, 154.
Tulip Tree, Ashby, 56.
Turville Family, 162.

ULLESTHORPE, 262, 263.
Uppingham, 189.
Uxbridge, Meeting of Charles and Parliament, 81.

WAPENBURY, 114.
Warwick, 106.
,, Castle, 80.
,, St. Mary's Church, 110.

Warwickshire Scenery, 2.
Watford Court, 63.
Watling Street, 1, 264.
Watson of Rockingham, 185.
Wat Tyler, 251.
Welford Church, 164.
Weston by Welland, 176.
Whitley Abbey, 134.
Wigston Magna, 85.

Wing Village, 196.
Winter of Huddington, 46.
Wolsey, 43.
Wolston, 89, 259.
  ,,   Church, 260.
Wright, John, 47.
Wycliffe, John, 250.

YOUNG, ENSIGN, 78

www.ingramcontent.com/pod-product-compliance
Lightning Source LLC
Chambersburg PA
CBHW022335230426
43664CB00040B/1064